STEVE BACKLUND

WITH JULIE MUSTARD
entries by Jared Cullop, Levi Hug, and Jaz Jacob

CRUCIAL MOMENTS

LEARNING TO SEE GOD IN THE MIDDLE OF DIFFICULTIES

Cover Design : Tyler Vaughn/ JCI Marketing
Cover Layout/ Interior Design and Formatting : Robert Schwendenmann/ JCI Marketing
JCI Marketing, Redding CA www.jcimarketing.com
Special Assistance by: Elizabeth Preece, Melissa Amato, Julie Heth, Joellah Lutz, and
Daniel Newton

ISBN: 978-0-9894725-2-4

CRUCIAL MOMENTS

CONTENTS

DEVOTIONALS page

ABOUT THE AUTHORS

Steve Backlund

Steve Backlund was a senior pastor for seventeen years before joining the team at Bethel Church in Redding, California, in 2008. Steve is a revivalist teacher who calls people to higher perspectives through believing truth. At Bethel Church, he teaches leadership development in both the ministry school and through Global Legacy's Leadership Development online school. Steve and his wife, Wendy are also the founders of Igniting Hope Ministries, which emphasizes joy, hope, and victorious mindsets through books, audio messages, and their extensive travel.

Julie Mustard, *Intern 2012-2013*

Prior to moving to Redding, CA, to attend BSSM, Julie engaged in a range of ministry and life experiences including starting an orphanage in Africa, writing books and curriculum, directing international missions camps, and teaching high school English in her home state of Texas. She is passionate about healthy relationships, people walking in the fullness of their identity in Christ, and has a heart to see people transformed inside and out in order to become the leaders and releasers of the Kingdom that God designed them to be. Julie works for Bethel Church in the Global Legacy Department and for Igniting Hope Ministries as an associate to Steve Backlund. She is also an itinerate minister with Bethel Activation Ministry (BAM).

Jared Cullop, *Intern 2012-2013*

Born in East Tennessee, Jared has since traveled the world with his wife, Erin, and kids, participating in YWAM, and moved to California to attend Bethel School of Supernatural Ministry (BSSM). He is a mentor in BSSM, offering an Entrepreneur Internship where he seeks to impart a true vision of hope-filled Kingdom Business by giving his interns full access to all decisions and meetings regarding his Redding, CA-based web design and marketing business, JCI Marketing.

Levi Hug, *Intern 2012-2013*

Levi is an entrepreneur who carries a contagious passion for global revival. He loves equipping those around him with mindsets that catalyze & sustain positive transformation. A graduate of Bethel School of Supernatural Ministry and Heidi Baker's Harvest School, Levi currently operates a business in the Pacific Northwest and travels, ministering the gospel around the world.

Jaz Jacob, *Intern 2012-2013*

Jaz is a world-renown worship leader and songwriter who has a heart to see the nations step into intimacy and a lifestyle of worship. Born and raised in Spain, Jaz spent many years sowing into several ministries and organizations. In addition to ministry in Spain, Jaz travels as a conference speaker and worship leader. She believes that signs and wonders are for today and sees the Kingdom expanded everywhere she goes. She carries hope, joy, and freedom from religiosity. She is passionate about seeing people step into their identity as children of God and live the life Jesus lived and called us to follow.

Jared, Levi, Steve, Jaz, and Julie

FOREWORD

by Steve Backlund

What are the most crucial moments of our Christian life? Is it when we have goose bumps on our goose bumps in a worship service? Is it when God uses us wonderfully to change a life? Could it be when we attend meetings where a special outpouring of the Holy Spirit is occurring? While these are important times for us, I believe other seemingly non-exciting moments are more crucial for our growth and advancement. What are they? I believe they are the apparent negative occurrences that happen to us. Our response to them will either catapult us into greater dimensions of life and influence or into more hopelessness and limitation. We have a choice to make when we face problems. This book is designed to release grace, higher perspectives, and wisdom for you to choose greater life-releasing responses to difficulties than ever before.

The contents of Crucial Moments were inspired by an experience of one of its authors, Levi Hug. When Levi would share the gospel with someone, and they said, "I am an atheist," he would see this as a problem, not an opportunity. He would move into non-victorious beliefs. His remedy to this "problem" was to say to someone proclaiming atheism, "Oh really, that is so exciting! God always shows up when I am around an atheist!" He realized he could not think a lie if he was speaking the truth. As a result of this strategy, Levi has had some incredible encounters with atheists (some whom are now former atheists!).

We have taken the phrase "Oh really, that is so exciting; God always shows up when . . . " and applied it to over 50 common negative moments to help us see our problems as opportunities to grasp how big our God is. You will definitely relate to many of the scenarios we present.

The concepts in Crucial Moments are not simply positive thinking techniques, but are rooted in Scriptural promises. And there is probably no greater promise regarding life's challenges than Romans 8:28. "And we know that all things work together for good to those who love God, to those who are the called according to His purpose." This is astonishing. No matter what happens to us or is done by us, He can supernaturally turn it for good as we turn our hearts to Him. This truth sets the foundation for what is shared in the book. It opens us up to see the bigger picture regarding challenges we face – and Crucial Moments is designed to cause us to see problems as possibilities like never before.

I so enjoyed working with Julie, Jared, Jaz, and Levi on this book. Each of their life experiences and insights contributed significantly. Julie is a great writer and has powerful insight into healthy relationships. Jared is a kingdom businessman who thinks like few others. Levi is an "encouragement machine" who blesses everyone around him with his simple, but profound revelations. And Jaz is a unique combination of worshiper and teacher who brings heaven's realities and insight to earth.

Be blessed as you read Crucial Moments.

Steve Backlund
Igniting Hope Ministries

1 YOUR HOUSE IS A MESS WHEN PEOPLE COME OVER

CRUCIAL MOMENT

The doorbell rings. Who could this be? You open the door and see your pastors, Bill and Sharon. Bill says, "We were in the area and thought we would stop by." You are excited to see them, so you invite them in. As they step through the door, you think to yourself, "Oh no, our house is a disaster!" There are plates and food scraps in the living room, the sink (which you can see from the front door) is full of dishes, and the bathroom has not been cleaned since the grandkids were over. You are fighting feelings of embarrassment, but this is a real opportunity for you to go to the next level in your life.

WHAT TO GET EXCITED ABOUT

- You get to joyfully reveal to the world that you are not perfect.
- You have the opportunity to reaffirm your true identity as an organized person who is just having a disorganized experience.
- This is a chance to be more motivated in getting a plan for greater order in your life.

STRENGTH THROUGH SCRIPTURE

- **2 Timothy 1:7** "For God has not given us a spirit of fear, but of power and of love and of a sound mind."
- **Philippians 4:4** "Rejoice in the Lord always. Again I will say, rejoice!"
- **Colossians 3:15** "And let the peace of God rule in your hearts, to which also you were called in one body; and be thankful."

PRACTICAL WISDOM

1. *Pursue excellence, but avoid the perfectionistic spirit* – Perfectionism wants to control all the little details of our lives, while excellence is doing something in an outstanding way. A person of excellence tends to be more relaxed and releases peace in the midst of trying moments, while the perfectionist has to have everything just right, creating an atmosphere of anxiety and a fear of failure.

2. *Value relationships above things* – If your house is a mess or something does not look nice, it is probable one or more other family members have contributed. This reality can certainly create frustration in relationships, but as we purpose to live a life prioritizing healthy relationships above external appearances, we will live with less stress and relationship breakdowns. Yes, we may need to have some frank discussions about family responsibilities, but we must avoid reactive and negative attitudes which are destructive to our closest relationships.

3. *Take steps to be more proactive and be better organized* – Those who learn how to order their lives and plan ahead will experience much less stress and frustration. Here are some small things which make a big a difference: 1) Clean things up daily before relaxing or having fun. 2) Do major organizing and cleaning in your home twice a year. 3) Have regular planning meetings with family to proactively prepare for upcoming happenings and to discuss family responsibilities.

DECLARATIONS

- God always shows up when people come over and my house is messy.
- I am a confident and secure person.
- I am a person of excellence, but the spirit of perfection is far from me.

YOUR ADULT CHILD IS MAKING VERY POOR DECISIONS

CRUCIAL MOMENT

It has happened to many parents. Their grown children are scaring them with the choices they are making. It is so difficult to watch, and it hurts your heart each and every time. If making poor decisions for their own life wasn't bad enough, there are children involved - your grandchildren! This behavior has also begun to affect your finances greatly. Just when it seems to be getting better, another crisis emerges. This is certainly a challenging situation, and one that gives you an opportunity to see God show up in powerful ways.

WHAT TO GET EXCITED ABOUT

- You have the opportunity to learn how to walk in the joy and peace of the Lord when people you love are making poor choices.
- You get to learn how to keep loving and believing in a family member without enabling his or her bad choices.
- You get to overcome any shame or condemnation which exists in your parent-child relationship.

STRENGTH THROUGH SCRIPTURE

- **1 Corinthians 10:13** "No temptation (trial) has overtaken you except such as is common to man; but God is faithful, who will not allow you to be tempted beyond what you are able, but with the temptation will also make the way of escape, that you may be able to bear it."
- **Proverbs 22:6** "Train up a child in the way he should go, and when he is old he will not depart from it."
- **James 5:16** "The effective, fervent prayer of a righteous man avails much."

PRACTICAL WISDOM

1. *Take your prayer life to the next level* – When our loved ones are making poor decisions, it is certainly a challenge to us emotionally. The good news is this: God's grace to us increases in proportion to the degree of the problems around us (see Romans 5:20). And there is great grace available to help us overcome fear, shame, anger, and other such emotions. This grace will lead our prayer lives beyond begging and pleading into a place where we find peace in the storm. Our peace will be a great weapon to bring victory.

2. *Get a good process in deciding how much you are to help* – There are two extremes concerning helping an adult child who is making bad choices. On one side, we can take full responsibility for their lives and become their "savior," while on the other side, we can disconnect from them until they get their lives together. The answer will probably be somewhere in between. The key is to avoid emotion-driven decisions. One way to do this is to include wise people in our decision making process.

3. *Believe God has a great solution* – Know this: our hopelessness about a problem is a bigger problem than the problem. One of our main battles is to believe God has a solution. Once we believe there is a direction for us, then that direction will be released to us.

DECLARATIONS

• God always shows up when my family members are making poor decisions.

• My prayers are powerful and effective for my family members.

• I make good decisions concerning how much to help my grown children.

YOU GAINED MORE WEIGHT THAN YOU THOUGHT

CRUCIAL MOMENT

Over the years, everyone sees changes in their bodies. People have weight variances for all kinds of reasons, but there is a certain sense of dread when you step on the scale after a period of time where you have not taken the best care of yourself. For whatever reason, your physical health has not been a priority, and when that number comes up on that digital screen, it becomes real - you gained more weight than you thought. In this crucial moment you get to decide whether to react or respond.

WHAT TO GET EXCITED ABOUT

- You get to learn how to make powerful decisions about food and your body by learning self-fontrol to a whole new level.
- You have the opportunity to understand how your body is a temple of the Holy Spirit designed to last 120+ years.
- This is a chance to strengthen positive beliefs about yourself, even when you seem to be failing.

STRENGTH THROUGH SCRIPTURE

- **1 Corinthians 6:12-14** "All things are lawful for me, but all things are not helpful. All things are lawful for me, but I will not be brought under the power of any."
- **I Corinthians 6:19** "Or do you not know that your body is the temple of the Holy Spirit who is in you, whom you have from God and your are not your own?"
- **Galatians 5:22 - 24** "But the fruit of the Spirit is love, joy, peace, longsuffering, kindness, goodness, faithfulness, gentleness, self-control. Against such there is no law. And those who are Christ's have crucified the flesh with its passions and desires"

PRACTICAL WISDOM

1. *Focus on getting healthy not just losing weight* – The saying, "The scale is just a number, not an indicator of health," can be helpful. Just because someone is skinny or weighs very little does not mean they are healthy. While obesity is an issue of weight loss, it is more important to focus on getting healthy as a lifestyle instead of losing weight. In doing this, you will avoid fad diets based on results, and implement life changes that will stick with you beyond the number on the scale.

2. *Find a support system* – Historically, having a weight problem is accepted in the church. It is overlooked and often not talked about. Programs like AA have been successful in bringing breakthrough to alcoholics because there is a support system in place to make sure members are successful. It is no different when it comes to losing weight and maintaining good health. Find peers who are living a healthy lifestyle who you can give permission to speak into your life and encourage you on your health journey.

3. *Invest in your health* – You only have one body, and it has to last you forever. You invest money in temporary things all the time, so why not invest money in your health? Consider buying one or more of the following: a juicer, a consultation with a nutritionist, or a gym membership. Make a plan for making that investment see some return. It is worth the money to live a long and healthy life. Investments can also be made in your identity beliefs regarding your weight. Making a plan to invest in speaking positive declarations over yourself and avoid partnering with discouragement in areas such as weight problems.

DECLARATIONS

- God always shows up when I realize that I gained more weight than I thought.
- I walk in divine health and actively take care of my physical body.
- I am a fat-burning machine.

YOUR JOB DOESN'T FEEL AS SPIRITUAL AS THOSE IN MINISTRY

CRUCIAL MOMENT

You love everything about your job; you were born for it. Sometimes, however, you are challenged with the mindset that your work in the marketplace is not as spiritual as people who are in ministry. Because you are not saving souls, healing the sick, or raising the dead, you feel your job is not as important to God. When you have a busy day filled with meetings, projects and writing emails, it can feel insignificant and it can be tempting to think that those in full-time ministry have a greater call or gifting on their lives. In moments like these, we seize our chance and believe God wants to show how big he really is.

WHAT TO GET EXCITED ABOUT

- You get to be a catalyst of breakthrough to the cultural mindsets of many Christians who work in the marketplace.
- You have the opportunity to influence individuals that people in ministry may never have the opportunity to reach.
- This is a chance to strengthen the gifting on your life through faithfulness.

STRENGTH THROUGH SCRIPTURE

- **Hebrews 10:23** "Let us hold fast the confession of our hope without wavering, for He who promised is faithful."
- **James 1:3** "The testing of your faith produces endurance."
- **1 Corinthians 3:16** "You are God's temple and God's spirit dwells in you."

PRACTICAL WISDOM

1. *Believe God is with you at work* - No matter what kind of job you have, God is with you at work. There is no such thing as a sacred job or a secular job. If you are part of the Kingdom of God, then you are called to bring the Kingdom into your workplace. What you believe is what will manifest. If you believe your job is changing the world, then your job is changing the world.

2. *Prophesy over yourself* - Getting God's perspective over our lives helps us live from a place of our identity rather than having to get everything right. As you declare the truth of who God says you are, you create a powerful world of inner success that will manifest in your life. This will help you to stop focusing on outward things to validate your success.

3. *Feed daily on the truth that God's glory is in you* - We are all created to display His nature on the earth and the same spirit that raised Christ from the dead dwells in you. Jesus not only proclaimed that He was the son of God, He knew it. Believe that the world needs you. Remind yourself daily of what your job is doing for the Kingdom.

DECLARATIONS

- God always shows up when my job feels less spiritual than those in full-time ministry

- I am a success in everything I put my hand to do

- I bring a hope and future to everyone around me

CRUCIAL MOMENT

You tossed and turned in bed for hours unable to sleep and finally dozed off a couple of hours before your alarm went off. Aware that you have a full day ahead of you with family responsibilities, meetings, and decisions, you can feel a bad attitude rising up within you. You know that you need to get your act together, but you're simply physically beat. What do you do?

WHAT TO GET EXCITED ABOUT

- You get to see evidence of the fruits of the Spirit in your life that you normally wouldn't see.
- You have the opportunity to see how God renews your strength.
- This is a chance to grow in your ability to rely on God and see Him show up in unexpected ways.

STRENGTH THROUGH SCRIPTURE

- **2 Corinthians 12:9** "My grace is sufficient for you, for my power is made perfect in weakness."
- **Isaiah 40:31** "But those who wait on the Lord shall renew their strength; They shall mount up with wings like eagles, they shall run and not be weary, They shall walk and not faint."
- **Ephesians 3:20** "Now to Him who is able to do exceedingly abundantly above all that we ask or think, according to the power that works in us"

PRACTICAL WISDOM

1. *Trust God and choose to get excited about how He's going to use you* - We have a promise that when we trust Him, He will renew our strength. So, quiet your mind and become aware of His presence. As you wait and trust, know He will renew your strength. When we read through Scripture, God tends to follow a pattern of choosing the least adequate, the downcast, the too old, the too young or . . . the too tired! So, as you quiet your mind, ask the Holy Spirit for creative ideas. Instead of focusing on your lack, allow yourself to get excited about how you being tired makes you a perfect target for God to use you!

2. *Expect to have a great day when you wake up tired* - Staying positive and expectant will already give you a running start in your day. He is able to do exceedingly more than we ask or think, so think of what an amazing day it's going to be and expect Him to do exceedingly abundantly more. Expectation is the same as faith and when we expect good things, we give God something to work with.

3. *Ask other people for a helping hand* – Being tired is the perfect opportunity to rely on the body of Christ and allow God to use others. Ask God to bring people to mind that might be able to help you in certain situations. Asking other people for help doesn't mean you have less faith or that you are less spiritual as God loves to unite people and use His body as a whole!

DECLARATIONS

- God always shows up when I'm tired.
- When I'm tired, God surprises me with supernatural energy and brings the perfect people my way to help me.
- God loves using me and partnering with me, especially when I'm tired or needing rest!

CRUCIAL MOMENT

After searching the scriptures you've come to believe that it is God's nature and will to heal everyone. You are passionately pursuing healing, and you along with others on the prayer team have spent long periods of time praying for Sally who has been diagnosed with cancer. It's Sunday morning and Sally is waiting in line for prayer. She is in severe pain and desperate for relief. When she comes to you, your mind is flooded with all the times you've prayed and yet "nothing happened." You hope someone else will pray for her, but it's too late as she's right in front of you.

WHAT TO GET EXCITED ABOUT

- You get to practice placing the roots of your beliefs in God's Word instead of your experience.
- You have the opportunity to grow in love, discovering new levels of God's compassion.
- This is a chance to be a part of Sally's story, knowing that the greater the resistance faced, the sweeter her victory will taste.

STRENGTH THROUGH SCRIPTURE

- **Mark 16:18** "They will lay hands on the sick, and they will recover."
- **Luke 8:43** "Now a woman, having a flow of blood for twelve years, who had spent all her livelihood on physicians and could not be healed by any, came from behind and touched the border of His garment. And immediately her flow of blood stopped."
- **1 John 2:6** "He who says he abides in Him [Jesus] ought himself also to walk just as He walked."

PRACTICAL WISDOM

1. *Resolve to always speak words of life and hope* - Jesus healed everyone who came to Him regardless of their level of faith, never implying that they didn't have enough faith to receive healing. Instead of looking for an explanation for Sally's circumstances, choose to speak words that will strengthen her. Try saying things like, "Sally, it is always a privilege to pray for you. We're in this together." or "Sally, you have tremendous faith."

2. *Determine that your beliefs will not be dictated by your experience but by God's Word* - When our experience doesn't line up with what God's Word says to be true, we often adjust the truth to make ourselves more comfortable with our circumstances. This can lead to creating doctrines such as "It's not God's will to heal everyone," or "God sometimes allows sickness to remain in order to teach people character." Let's be honest, choosing faith in the face of situations like Sally's can feel awkward. But, instead of getting frustrated by your lack of control and answers, choose to embrace mystery in this moment and believe God's promises in the face of negative circumstances.

3. *Take time in private to pray for "more" of God* - We cannot settle for an experience which is not in line with the experience of Jesus Christ. He said if we believe in Him we would do what He did and even "greater things" (John 14:12). Jesus is the prototype of what a "normal Christian" is supposed to look like. Use the uncomfortable experience you've had with Sally for fuel in your prayer closet. Take Sally before the Lord, and believe for a deeper encounter with Him. "Father, I must know You more because Jesus would have healed Sally when He walked the earth. Holy Spirit, fill me to a greater degree so I can represent Your nature more clearly."

DECLARATIONS

• God always shows up when I pray for people with long-standing and unresolved health issues.

• Every time I pray something happens whether people "feel it" or not.

• I live by faith not by experience.

7

YOU NEED TO MAKE A DECISION, BUT ARE HAVING "ANALYSIS PARALYSIS"

CRUCIAL MOMENT

It's decision time and you are a mess. You have no idea what to do. "Analysis Paralysis" has engulfed your brain. The deadline for an important decision is looming, creeping ever closer. You make spreadsheets, argue every angle within your head, and still can't seem to hold on to a conclusion for more than thirty minutes at a time. You have asked for counsel from all of your wise friends, yet there is no agreement amongst them. Anxiety and fear are knocking at your door, making it hard to think clearly. A decision has to be made but you feel paralyzed.

WHAT TO GET EXCITED ABOUT

- You get to see how God loves to highlight His kids to the world through their amazing decisions and choices.
- You have the opportunity to tap into one of the most profound promises in the Bible- that God will give us wisdom if we ask Him for it.
- This is a chance to look to the past, to your previous testimonies and those of others, and apply those lessons to this new situation.

STRENGTH THROUGH SCRIPTURE

- **Isaiah 30:21** "Your ears shall hear a word behind you, saying, 'This is the way, walk in it,' Whenever you turn to the right hand, or whenever you turn to the left."
- **Psalm 51:6** "Behold, You desire truth in the inward parts, and in the hidden part You will make me to know wisdom."
- **James 1:5** "If any of you lacks wisdom, let him ask of God, who gives to all liberally and without reproach, and it will be given to him."

PRACTICAL WISDOM

1. *Ask God in the secret place* – God speaks to us through dreams, other people, our imaginations and visions, and through His Word. When making a decision, it's good to work out your feelings about each option with God, but be sure to give much more time in prayer to listening. Start out with thanksgiving and praise. Remember, follow your peace and favor by paying attention to what Holy Spirit IS saying.

2. *Ask God for wisdom* – Wisdom is always good, and He always gives it. If you feel like you are not getting much of a solid answer from God in your special time with Him, maybe He wants to see what you come up with on your own. In this case, an extra helping of wisdom and discernment is a good idea.

3. *Enlist the counsel of fathers and mothers in your life* – We are to live life in community for a reason - so we can help each other through shared wisdom and testimony. Find someone in your life who walks closely with God and seems to be an incredible decision maker. Present your situation to them objectively and don't be offended if they ask you lots of questions.

DECLARATIONS

- God always shows up when I face an important, difficult decision.
- There is ALWAYS a solution.
- I make incredible decisions, and my ability to do so is an encouragement and testimony to others.

CRUCIAL MOMENT

You find yourself all alone at the end of a difficult day. You turn on the computer to check the latest scores, see what is happening in the news, and all of a sudden your thoughts begin to go in a different direction. You wonder how easy it would be to access pornography. You didn't sit down with this intention, but now you're tempted. Whether you're male or female, single or married, this is a crucial moment that many of us face. Everything you could ever imagine is viewable within just a few keystrokes. You hear the lies that no one will ever find out, that it won't really hurt your heart. You start to fantasize about what could soon be on your screen.

WHAT TO GET EXCITED ABOUT

- You get to ask God for strength to remain pure. It's hard for us to imagine, but Jesus dealt with temptations too. And as a man, He did not sin.
- You have the opportunity to realize our sex drive was put into us to accompany deep covenant relationship. By choosing not to defile that drive, you are sowing into a deep, passionate intimacy with your spouse, whether now or in the future.
- This is a chance to choose to keep yourself pure before God, and your relationship with Him will grow as a result!

STRENGTH THROUGH SCRIPTURE

- **Hebrews 4:15** "For we do not have a High Priest who cannot sympathize with our weaknesses, but was in all points tempted as we are, yet without sin."

- **Philippians 4:8** "Finally, brethren, whatever things are true, whatever things are noble, whatever things are just, whatever things are pure, whatever things are lovely, whatever things are of good report, if there is any virtue and if there is anything praiseworthy—meditate on these things."

- **1 Corinthians 6:18-20** "Flee sexual immorality. Every sin that a man does is outside the body, but he who commits sexual immorality sins against his own body. Or do you not know that your body is the temple of the Holy Spirit who is in you, whom you have from God, and you are not your own? For you were bought at a price; therefore glorify God in your body and in your spirit, which are God's."

PRACTICAL WISDOM

1. *Have an "out"*– Have a game plan previously set for when this time comes. Maybe you praise God in that time, forcing temptation to leave. Simply hit some other keys that pull up some amazing worship music.

2. *Find a confidant* – It's important that we have someone to talk about the temptations we face behind closed doors. It is important to find someone who will challenge you to a life of vision, purity, integrity, and not someone who simply excuses what you are doing because of their own lack of victory in this area. Someone cannot help you get out of a pit that they are in too. As we consider pursuing others, it is important to know it is not a sign of weakness to do so; rather, it is a sign of strength to invite others to help. The very act of bringing our struggle out of secrecy into the light of accountability in relationship is an act of courage and is a great key to breakthrough.

3. *Love the faceless many who are involved in making pornography or are the victims of sex trafficking* – If we can get a love for the group of those trapped in the industry as a whole, then we can see the love of God for each of them, a love that makes the lies and temptations melt away for us. You can get good insight into the real evil and degrading truth behind the porn industry, as well as join accountability groups and programs, on websites such as www.xxxchurch.com and www.covenanteyes.com.

DECLARATIONS

- God always shows up when I need His strength and truth to fight temptation.
- I pursue and find great people to be in my life to help me walk in incredible purity.
- I am more fulfilled and satisfied concerning my sex life than anything I will ever see on a computer screen.

YOUR CHILDREN'S BEHAVIOR EMBARRASSES YOU

CRUCIAL MOMENT

Your child throws a tantrum in a very public place, exhibits extremely selfish behavior when playing with the children of someone you respect, or fails at something we think every child should do well. Which parent has not had a child do at least one of these things? Children are notorious for having poor timing in doing things which can be embarrassing for their parents. While all good parents want their children to be exemplary children, these embarrassing moments are crucial moments in our lives and in the lives of our children.

WHAT TO GET EXCITED ABOUT

*   You get to break off any people-pleasing spirit that may be in your life.
*   You have the opportunity to prioritize your heart connection with your child over what people think about you.
*   This is a chance to learn to laugh and lighten up in uncomfortable situations.

STRENGTH THROUGH SCRIPTURE

*   **1 Samuel 16:7** "Man looks at the outward appearance, but the Lord looks at the heart."
*   **Proverbs 29:25** "The fear of man brings a snare, but whoever trusts in the Lord shall be safe."
*   **1 John 4:18** "There is no fear in love; but perfect love casts out fear."

PRACTICAL WISDOM

1. *Resist the "super parent" syndrome* – Our society puts pressure on parents to have children who are the smartest, the most attractive, the most talented, the best athletes, and who are seen as exceptional. These desires can create an unhealthy emphasis on outward appearances and accomplishments, which can create a performance-based parent-child relationship (rather than one based on a good heart connection). One way to defeat the "super parent" syndrome is to put more emphasis on the child's heart attitudes than on outward performance or appearance.

2. *Declare war on the fear of embarrassment* – An excessive desire to avoid embarrassing ourselves (or looking stupid to others) hinders many from freedom in life. The fear of looking like a failure fuels these restrictive mindsets. God invites all of us to become successful on the inside when we don't look successful on the outside (and provides the grace to do so). As we grow in inward success, the need for people's approval will grow less and less.

3. *Grow in your parenting skills* – Never stop learning how to be more effective as a parent. Some of our children's embarrassing behavior will be a wake-up call for us to make a greater emphasis in our parent-child relationship. God has wisdom and solutions for every situation we face. Additionally, there are books, seminars, and various other resources available for growing your parenting and communication skills.

DECLARATIONS

- God always shows up when my children do embarrassing things.

- I am a great parent who responds with love and wisdom to whatever my child does.

- I am a confident person, and the fear of man is far from me.

10 AN INFLUENTIAL PERSON HAS A NEGATIVE OPINION OF YOU

CRUCIAL MOMENT

A key person in your life does not see you as highly as you think he should. Whenever you walk by him, he looks at you and seemingly disregards you. He does not place as much value on you as he does to others, and these "others" have some issues in their lives that are being either ignored or overlooked. In the relationship, you feel you are being labeled as something you believe you are not. This person seems to have his favorites, and you are not one of them. You feel stuck, misunderstood, and frustrated. Praise God! This is a crucial moment which could be a launching pad into your life purpose!

WHAT TO GET EXCITED ABOUT

- You get to put your trust in God, and not in man.
- You have the opportunity to implement the truth that your response to something is almost always more important than the something.
- This is a chance to strengthen the truth that you are not a victim of the perceptions others have of you.

STRENGTH THROUGH SCRIPTURE

Luke 2:52 "And Jesus increased in wisdom and stature, and in favor with God and men."

Acts 15:38 "But Paul insisted that they should not take (Mark) with them who had departed from them in Pamphylia, and had not gone with them to the work."

2 Timothy 4:11 "Get Mark and bring him with you, for he is useful to me for ministry."

PRACTICAL WISDOM

1. *Celebrate and carry out with excellence the opportunities you DO have* – Too often we focus on what is NOT happening in our lives rather than what is happening. Do you have a job? Many people don't. Do you have opportunities to minister? Others would love to do what you do. Someone's negative opinion of us may seem to block doors from opening, but there are doors which are open now. As you embrace the opportunities you have with excellence and enthusiasm, it increases the likelihood of other doors opening (regardless of what influential people think of you).

2. *Focus more on becoming something rather than on doing something* – Many people in the Bible worked through negative opinions of influential people by focusing more on their inner world than their outer world. In Joseph's situation, he prospered in prison despite being falsely thought to be a rapist by influential people. He did not become bitter, but he became better as a person and eventually great doors opened for him.

3. *Receive God's wisdom for your specific situation* – No two circumstances are alike when it comes to this topic. The first key to hearing God's wisdom for you is to overcome any sense that you are a victim of this person's opinion of you. Next, consider what you are to do. Sometimes we are to meet with the person, ask good questions, and share our heart. Other times we are to trust God and do nothing. Also, we must be aware that there will times when the person's opinion is right, and we need to seek to make changes in our lives. Finally, there will be those times when we are to distance ourselves from the person. God will help you know what to do.

DECLARATIONS

- God always shows up when influential people have a negative opinion of me.

- I am not held back by the opinions of others.

- I always know what to do when there is a relationship challenge in my life.

11 SHARING JESUS WITH AN ATHEIST

CRUCIAL MOMENT

I love to share the Gospel in everyday-life situations and I've noticed people often react to the Good News by immediately becoming defensive. These defenses are often expressed as verbal arguments validating their non-candidacy for the Gospel. In past scenarios, I would get uncomfortable and even scared when someone would say to me, "I am an Atheist." I've learned that when someone responds to the Gospel with the argument of, "I'm an Atheist" they are inviting me to: 1) argue with them or 2) leave them alone. I've never seen arguing bring positive results, and leaving people alone usually does nothing. I'd like to propose a third option of response in such situations—getting excited. Instead of arguing or ignoring I choose to get excited in these crucial moments, because God always shows up when I meet atheists!

WHAT TO GET EXCITED ABOUT

- You get to grow in showing love in action, boldness, and faith.
- This is an opportunity to love a soul that is one belief away from becoming a new creation in Christ.
- This is a chance to demolish an argument that has set itself up against the knowledge of God, simply through love.

STRENGTH THROUGH SCRIPTURE

- **2 Corinthians 10:3-5** "For though we walk in the flesh, we do not war according to the flesh. For the weapons of our warfare are not carnal but mighty in God for pulling down strongholds, casting down arguments and every high thing that exalts itself against the knowledge of God, bringing every thought into captivity to the obedience of Christ"
- **1 Samuel 17:48** "So it was when the Philistine arose and came and drew near to meet David, that David hurried and ran quickly toward the battle line to meet the Philistine [Goliath]."
- **1 Timothy 2:4** "[God] desires all men to be saved and to come to the knowledge of the truth."

PRACTICAL WISDOM

1. *Resolve to always love people* - Many times when we encounter people who are bound by lies, it is easy to personalize their arguments, not realizing our battle is never against people. Our arguments are against lying arguments that are keeping them bound. When we understand people are never our enemy, but rather the lies they believe, we free ourselves to always love no matter what we experience from those around us.

2. *Know the battle you are fighting* - 2 Corinthians 10:3-5 reveals a great key to spiritual warfare—winning the battle in our own thought lives. This concept is important to understand when trying to help those around us who may be bound by lies. Love-driven excitement is a weapon that can be mighty in God for pulling down strongholds in those around us. In doing this, we can dismantle arguments in people's minds without ever arguing with them.

3. *Have fun* - For many, evangelism can be a topic surrounded by anxiety and pressure, but people are attracted to freedom and authenticity. So, be yourself, soak in the Spirit, experience God's joy, and have fun! Get excited when you meet atheists because this type of response is usually not expected by them. Responding with overflowing love and excitement often begins to dismantle their strongholds and preconceived notions before you've even said anything about the Gospel.

DECLARATIONS

• Jesus loves atheists!

• God always shows up when I meet Atheists, Agnostics, Buddhists, Muslims, Shamans, or any other "non-Gospel candidates."

• Everyone (including atheists) is longing to know Jesus.

CRUCIAL MOMENT

Have you ever put your blood, sweat, and tears into a project just to see someone else get credit for it? It can feel defeating and deflating to think that you worked so hard on something and no one noticed; or worse, someone else takes credit for it. Imagine spearheading a great idea on the job and working hard to make it happen. It has turned into a huge success, but when senior management visits your department, your overseer minimizes your efforts, taking the credit. You feel under-valued and used. Your opinion of your manager is quickly waning and your passion for work is gone. Instead of giving in to these negative emotions, take this crucial moment as opportunity to see what God is doing on a whole different level.

WHAT TO GET EXCITED ABOUT

- You get to make someone else look like a genius and realize that God is your advocate.
- You have the opportunity to do everything for the Lord and not for the praise of men.
- This is a chance to understand that "hiddeness" is a training season for something bigger, so you get to walk in great assurance of an eternal reward knowing that God sees your hard work and gracious attitude.

STRENGTH THROUGH SCRIPTURE

- **Galatians 1:10** "For do I now persuade me or God? Or do I seek to please men? For if I still pleased men, I would not be a bondservant of Christ."
- **Proverbs 25:2** "It is the glory of God to conceal a matter, But the glory of kings is to search out a matter."
- **John 12:42-43** "The Pharisees…did not confess Him…for they loved the praise of men more than the praise of God.

PRACTICAL WISDOM

1. ***Don't take it personally*** – When someone else takes credit for your work, it can feel personal, but it is important to release the person from judgment and any sort of unforgiveness. Holding feelings of anger and bitterness towards them in the hope that it will make you feel better is like drinking poison and expecting them to die; it just isn't going to happen. If you do feel it was personal, be proactive about having a conversation with them to seek to understand their persective better.

2. ***Give credit away freely*** – Feeling you deserve something is a form of entitlement that leads down some dangerous paths. In these situations, instead of thinking you "deserve" something, why don't you try giving credit away to others. This is not flattery or manipulation, but an opportunity to support the efforts and accolades of other people. Being generous in your area of need will help you gain a higher perspective and cut off the spirit of entitlement.

3. ***Enjoy the cave*** – Most people want to be noticed and seen for the things they have accomplished, but there is a season of "cave time" that is part of our preparation for greater things. Pay attention to the season you are in. If you are noticing that you are being overlooked or someone else is getting credit for what you have done, maybe God is hiding you for a reason. Spend time in His Presence and hear His heart for you. You will find that your efforts do not go unnoticed when you realize God sees what you did in secret.

DECLARATIONS

- God always shows up when someone else gets credit for something I did.
- I love making people around me look like geniuses.
- I love seasons of hiddenness because they strengthen my character to prepare me to do great things.

13 YOU DON'T FEEL LIKE WORSHIPPING

CRUCIAL MOMENT

All of us go through times when we don't feel like worshipping. Sometimes it is the result of being tired or distracted. Other times, it is due to worry or disappointment about a situation we are facing, or maybe we simply just don't want to worship. Our heart of adoration toward God is an important part of maintaining our connection with Him. Whatever the situation, the emotion of not "feeling it" can be strong. It is during times like these that we get to make a decision to choose something greater than the emotion that is presented.

WHAT TO GET EXCITED ABOUT

- You get to be set free from negative thought patterns and discouraging feelings as you choose to worship.
- You have the opportunity to grow in your ability to see things from God's perspective as you worship.
- This is a chance to fulfill your God-given destiny! You were created to worship and will step into your identity as a worshipper as you declare who He is in the midst of your situation.

STRENGTH THROUGH SCRIPTURE

- **Psalm 103:1** "Praise the LORD, my soul; all my inmost being, praise His holy name."
- **Colossians 3:2** "Set your minds on things above, not on earthly things."
- **Psalm 34:1** "I will bless the LORD at all times; His praise shall continually be in my mouth."

PRACTICAL WISDOM

1. *Choose to put your mind on "things above"* - If you're worried or oppressed by something, choose to put your focus and attention on Him. When you worship, you choose to stop viewing things from an earthly perspective and start viewing things from His perspective. In 1 Samuel 22:5, the prophet Samuel told David: "Do not stay in the stronghold; but depart, and go to the land of Judah." Our negative thought patterns can form strongholds and the word, "Judah" literally means worship! In order to get victory from negative strongholds, it is vital to choose to go from patterns of thinking to places of worship.

2. *Be intentional about setting time aside to worship* – When do you least feel like worshipping? Is it when you are stuck in traffic? Or maybe it is when you are concerned about a certain person or situation? These are good times to intentionally stop and choose to worship. If your situation does not allow you to set time aside, take advantage of the time that you do have. Maybe you just have three minutes as you sit in your car in a parking lot, or a few seconds as you work around the house. Make these times "intentional worship times." Choosing to worship will make dull or stressful times fun.

3. *Schedule time to tell your soul to worship!* – Telling your soul to worship is as easy as telling yourself (out loud), "Worship soul!" Even King David, the greatest worshiper of all time, had to tell himself to do so (see Psalm 103:1). We can also do this in the least probable times: when you are tired, when things didn't turn out how you expected, when you just had a fight with your kids or spouse, etc. Times like these are good times to see things the way that God sees them and are therefore good times to choose to worship.

DECLARATIONS

- God always shows up when I don't feel like worshipping!
- As I worship, I acquire heaven's perspective over my life and situation, and I start seeing things as He sees them.
- When I worship, Jesus is glorified, heaven invades earth, and hell shakes in terror.

CRUCIAL MOMENT

You will be called up front to speak shortly. You are trying to fight off the feelings of anxiety but are having little success. Your mind rehearses past failures and thinks of the excellent speakers who are in the room. "What if I blank out? What if I don't make sense? What if I make a fool of myself?" It may be easier said than done, but relax and start rejoicing because this is a glorious crucial moment in your life.

WHAT TO GET EXCITED ABOUT

- You get to overcome the fear of man.

- You have the opportunity to conquer a fear many people face.

- This is a chance to have joy in the journey and not just when you experience complete victory in an area.

STRENGTH THROUGH SCRIPTURE

- **Acts 4:13** "Now when they saw the boldness of Peter and John, and perceived that they were uneducated and untrained men, they marveled. And they realized that they had been with Jesus."

- **Exodus 6:30** "But Moses said before the Lord, 'Behold, I am of uncircumcised lips, and how shall Pharaoh heed me?'"

- **Matthew 10:19-20** "But when they deliver you up, do not worry about how or what you should speak. For it will be given to you in that hour what you should speak. For it is not you who speak, but the Spirit of your Father who speaks in you . . .'"

PRACTICAL WISDOM

1. *Surrender your reputation to God* – There are moments in life where we are faced with an opportunity to surrender our reputation in a fresh way to God (and being insecure before speaking is one of those times). "Lord, I surrender my fear of failure to you. I release my reputation to you, and I declare that you are more important to me than what people think of me." As we yield our hearts to God in this way, it sets our life up for freedom, blessing, and influence.

2. *Realize love for others drives away fear* – "Perfect love casts out fear" (I John 4:18). A mother's love for a child would cause her to overcome the fear of a dangerous animal attempting to hurt her child. In the same way, truly wanting to strengthen those to whom you are speaking will greatly help in overcoming the fear of public speaking. Love causes us to get our eyes off ourselves and onto others; thus helping to neutralize our negative emotions.

3. *Learn these practical steps to relaxing when you speak* – 1) Share your battle with anxiety with someone and have them pray with you before you speak. 2) Take slow, deep breaths. 3) Start with a story or something you are very familiar with because you speak best what you know best. 4) Realize most speakers feel more nervous than they look, so you are in good company. 5) Focus on someone in the back of the room, on friendly faces, or on those who are most engaged. 6) Prepare well by memorizing key points that you will remember without notes (but still have notes in front of you just in case).

DECLARATIONS

- God always shows up when I am anxious about public speaking.

- I am a confident, influential, and joyful speaker.

- My love for people causes me to overcome my fear of speaking in front of them.

15 YOU GET A NEGATIVE DOCTOR'S REPORT

CRUCIAL MOMENT

Everyone knows the feeling of going in for a yearly checkup; it is not always fun. One day, I went in for a traditional check-up thinking everything was fine. What I left with was a report that could have caused my mind to go to a number of places filled with fear, hopelessness, and despair. To make it worse, both of my parents battled cancer and lost, and my mind immediately wanted to remember the pain of their diagnosis. Instead of giving in to those negative feelings, I decided to make a choice. I did not deny the existence of the report, but I was faced with a crucial moment in deciding how I would respond to it. You may have faced a similar situation, and been given an opportunity for God to show up on your behalf.

WHAT TO GET EXCITED ABOUT

- You get to see that Jesus loves to heal people. Every person who came to Jesus for healing was healed.
- You get the opportunity to see that a negative report is a chance to see how big our God is.
- This is a chance to stand firm in our faith and not worry.

STRENGTH THROUGH SCRIPTURE

- **Isaiah 53:5** "But He was pierced for our transgressions . . . by His stripes we are healed."
- **James 1:5** "But if any of you lacks wisdom, let him ask of God, who gives liberally and without reproach, and it will be given to him."
- **Psalm 30:2** "Lord, my God, I called to you for help and you healed me."

PRACTICAL WISDOM

1. *Believe the truth is greater than the report* – Modern medicine and doctors are indeed a gift from God, but often people take the results of test and reports as truth instead of facts. The facts may diagnose you with a disease, but the truth is that Jesus paid for that disease to be healed. Take time to write down every time in your life God has proven Himself more true than the facts and stand on these testimonies!

2. *Feast on Testimonies of Healing* – The word "testimony" means to "do it again." While you are believing for healing, celebrate the testimonies of other people who have been healed of the very thing you have been diagnosed with and claim it for yourself. Keeping a positive attitude and believing for the best through the process will be enhanced by focusing on the good.

3. *Refuse to Come Into Agreement with the Diagnosis* – One of the things that people tend to do when faced with a scary situation is to "own it." The premise for this thinking may be noble, but when you say things like "My disease keeps me from. . . " or "I am terminally ill," you unwittingly come into agreement with and possibly perpetuate the problem. I am not saying to be in denial, but be careful how you speak regarding the diagnosis.

DECLARATIONS

- God always shows up when I get a bad doctor's report.
- I am the healed one because Jesus paid for my complete healing.
- The truth of my faith is greater than the report.

16 THIS CHURCH MEETING SEEMS BORING

CRUCIAL MOMENT

"I'm bored!" Most parents have heard these infamous words from their children. Moms and dads often respond to this statement with ideas for enjoyable activities that the child had not considered. In a similar manner, we as God's spiritual children don't want to have feelings of boredom when we attend a church meeting. We want to experience something exciting and emotionally fulfilling. There is nothing wrong with these desires, but when feelings of boredom come, we have a crucial moment of great opportunity to grow and increase our influence.

WHAT TO GET EXCITED ABOUT

- You get to break off the addiction of needing outside stimuli to be enthusiastic and happy in life.

- You have the opportunity of learning to be a thermostat instead of a thermometer in your environments.

- You get to overcome any tendency to be critical of those leading the meeting; instead, you become a greater strength to them.

STRENGTH THROUGH SCRIPTURE

- **Colossians 3:23** "And whatever you do, do it heartily, as to the Lord and not to men."

- **Romans 12:10-12** "Be . . . not lagging in diligence, fervent in spirit, serving the Lord; rejoicing in hope, patient in tribulation, continuing steadfastly in prayer."

- **Psalm 37:4** "Delight yourself also in the Lord, and He shall give you the desires of your heart."

PRACTICAL WISDOM

1. *Decide to be a person of extraordinary enthusiasm* – Enthusiasm comes from the Greek word entheos, which means "to be full of the gods." This attitude can grow in us, and it is a key for growing in influence and having a good quality of life. Situations which lack excitement are our opportunity to build up our enthusiasm muscle.

2. *Purpose to be an incredible strength to the leaders around you* – Everyone wants to be the friend of the thriving leader, but few are the encouragers and helpers of those who do not have outward success. Most of us will have times in our lives where God calls us to be committed to ministries and leaders that are not as "exciting" as others. This dedication will help wean us from being emotion-driven in our attitudes and commitments.

3. *Consider if you are in a season of transition* – If we experience a long period of spiritual boredom and inner discontent, we need to consider if it is time for a change in our lives. We will obviously need to make sure we are not running from responsibility or from a time of growth, but chronic boredom can indicate we are getting ready for transition.

DECLARATIONS

- God always shows up when I start getting feelings of boredom in church.

- My enthusiasm is a thermostat improving every environment of which I am a part.

- I understand the times and seasons of my life, and I know what to do.

17 YOU RECOGNIZE A PATTERN OF GOSSIP IN YOUR LIFE

CRUCIAL MOMENT

Once again, the person who always messes up makes another mistake. You turn to your friend and say, "Bless his heart, he is so socially awkward." In this moment you realize something. For most of your life, you have been "perceptive" about people and events. It has never occurred to you that what you once called "discernment" could actually be gossip. Upon this realization, you begin to feel various conflicting emotions. Knowing that you do not want to be a gossip or have any part of it in your life, you are faced with a crucial moment to stay in this pattern or make a change for the better.

WHAT TO GET EXCITED ABOUT

- You get to address lifelong negative patterns in your life.
- You have the opportunity to become the greatest encourager you know.
- This is a chance to practice self-control and to bridle your tongue.

STRENGTH THROUGH SCRIPTURE

- **Psalm 34:13** "Keep your tongue from evil, and your lips from speaking deceit."
- **1 Corinthians 14:31** "For you can all prophesy one by one, that all may learn and all may be encouraged."
- **1 Thessalonians 5:11** "Therefore support each other and edify one another, just as you also are doing."

PRACTICAL WISDOM

1. *Go on a negativity fast* – You have the power of life and death in your tongue. It is important that you learn how to steward your life by stewarding your words. Now that you are aware of a pattern of gossip, keep track of the number of times per day that you think negative thoughts and go to war on them. Try reading Steve Backlund's book, Igniting Faith in 40 Days, and partake in the negativity fast. As you do, begin to feast on positivity.

2. *Get accountability with others* – It is a good idea to have accountability in your lives for many different things, so it makes sense to include others in your plan to stay far away from gossip. You don't want people to be the "Word Police", but having one or two people to help you be more aware of your words could be constructive. Give parameters for what this accountability looks like to set yourself up for success.

3. *Go on an encouragement rampage* – The best way to defeat gossip is to go on an encouragement rampage. Every time that you think in a judgmental way or find yourself talking negatively about someone, turn it into good. Instead of gossiping, bless the person, give them a prophetic word, or say something that builds them up instead of tearing them down.

DECLARATIONS

*   God always shows up when I recognize a pattern of gossip in my life.
*   I am the greatest encourager of others I know.
*   I prophesy life to everyone I meet.

18 YOU DON'T FEEL EXCITED WHEN HEARING A TESTIMONY

CRUCIAL MOMENT

A lady in your church approaches you in the lobby to tell you that last week her dog got healed of indigestion after she prayed for him. She's thrilled about what God has done, but this is one of many testimonies you've heard lately. You laugh and say a token, "Praise God," yet you know on the inside you are not sincere. Another guy gets up during sharing time and tells the congregation that his headache got healed during worship. You are happy for him, but honestly not super excited. Suddenly, you notice that your heart isn't responding like it once did. What happened? You feel numb. Where did that sense of "awe & wonder" go? Inside, you know you're facing a decision. Will you celebrate what God is doing, even when you're not feeling excited?

WHAT TO GET EXCITED ABOUT

- You get to learn something about God through every testimony you hear.
- You have the opportunity to make a perspective adjustment that is going to radically change your life.
- This is a chance to lead your emotions. Your choice to celebrate is not based on fluctuating feelings, but on a deeper understanding of what is happening in this crucial moment.

STRENGTH THROUGH SCRIPTURE

- **Psalm 119:14** "I have rejoiced in the way of Your testimonies, as much as in all riches."
- **Psalm 119:36** "Incline my heart to Your testimonies, and not to covetousness."
- **Psalm 119: 111** "Your testimonies I have taken as a heritage forever, for they are the rejoicing of my heart."

PRACTICAL WISDOM

1. **Make it a habit to instinctively celebrate good news** - Isn't it interesting that many who are quick to question good news will rarely question bad news? This is a symptom of a heart that is overcome with disappointment and defending itself against further pain. Jesus is the Healer of our bodies and our hearts. Let Him continually heal your heart from disappointment so you can instinctively rejoice like a child when encountering good news. The world will tell you, "Don't get your hopes up," but God is saying, "Get your hopes up in Me."

2. **Become a student of your heart's response to testimonies to monitor your spiritual health** - As a Christian it is vitally important to protect a healthy appetite for testimonies and to monitor our heart's response to them. Do they trigger rejoicing in us? The testimonies of God's acts, His miracles, and signs and wonders are living eternal entities which declare His never-changing nature. If we become numb to His testimonies, then we are in danger of becoming numb to Him.

3. **Jump start your excitement** - If you are not excited about a testimony, lead your heart into a state of excitement and rejoicing by saying things out loud such as "That's a miracle" or "Wait, wait, I didn't get it that time. You said what?" Rehearse the testimony by speaking it back to the person: "You're telling me that you had a migraine headache before worship and now it's gone!?" This intentionally captures the power of that testimony in the moment – don't miss this opportunity to encounter God through a testimony!

DECLARATIONS

- God always shows up when I realize I am not excited about a testimony.
- When I hear testimonies of God's goodness, people often assume by my response that I have just won the lottery (see Psalm 119:14).
- I love meditating on the testimonies of Jesus because they daily teach me about God's nature.

A POLITICIAN WHOSE BELIEFS OPPOSE YOURS IS ELECTED

CRUCIAL MOMENT

Despite all of your campaigning on Facebook, the signs in your yard, and the stickers on the back of your car, someone is elected to office with whom you strongly disagree. "How did God appoint THIS GUY? How on earth am I to honor HIM?" Well, the first step in deciding whether you will accept this happening is to ask yourself if you can you find a way to honor this person, or do you continue your campaign against them?

WHAT TO GET EXCITED ABOUT

- You get to see how God often uses stark contrasts as a way to bring entire countries back to Him.
- You have the opportunity to grow in standing for truth and justice while still walking in honor toward someone who opposes what you believe.
- This is a chance to see that God puts all the kings of the earth in place, and uses His people to shine His light.

STRENGTH THROUGH SCRIPTURE

- **Romans 13:1** "Let every soul be subject to the governing authorities. For there is no authority except from God, and the authorities that exist are appointed by God."
- **Proverbs 24:21** "My son, fear the Lord and the king; do not associate with those given to change."
- **1 Timothy 2:1-2** "Therefore I exhort first of all that supplications, prayers, intercessions, and giving of thanks be made for all men, for kings and all who are in authority, that we may lead a quiet and peaceable life in all godliness and reverence."

PRACTICAL WISDOM

1. *Remove the signs from your yard and bumper stickers from your car* – Even if the politician is undeniably against the views of God, once they are in power, we must not show disunity. We must not be divided as a nation. Plus, it's a chance to learn how to honor someone with whom you disagree. As we handle these situations with integrity, people will respect your stances in the future, and God will be glorified in your neighborhood.

2. *Become active* – If you live in a democracy, you have elected positions in your own community. If you don't feel called to occupy a position yourself, find someone whom you agree with and God is highlighting to you and support him or her, and find ways to listen to and honor those that have different agendas and opinions.

3. *Pray and intercede* – It is impossible for a Christian to pray, declare, and intercede and have nothing happen. Our prayers will make the difference. Even the wicked King Nebuchadnezzar had a life-changing encounter with the Lord in Daniel 4. Just like him, the leaders of today could be one prayer away from a similar experience.

DECLARATIONS

- God always shows up when I don't agree with those in my government.
- Politicians cannot stop the revival happening in my country!
- [Politician's name] wants to know God's heart for him, and will be used by powerfully by God while serving in office. I bless [politician] today.

20 YOU FEEL SCARED OR INSECURE

CRUCIAL MOMENT

When I was little and had to do something new such as climb the jungle gym or tie my shoes, I used to get scared and say between sobs, "I'm just a little girl!" Years later, even though I keep growing and getting older, when faced with a new challenge, I often find myself repeating these same words to God now: "God! I'm just a little girl!" You might not say these exact same words, but it may sound something like: "I'm too old," "I don't have enough money," or "I don't have what it takes." Statements like these can indicate that we are feeling fearful or insecure about the situation. Life is full of surprises that inevitably bring challenges and adjustments. How do you choose to face adjustments and challenges in which you might not feel brave or confident?

WHAT TO GET EXCITED ABOUT

- You get to grow in your level of trust in God and experience His love, which casts out all fear.
- You have the opportunity to grow in peace in situations that previously would have been stressful.
- This is a chance to see how His strength surpasses your weakness, and you get to see Him come through as you take brave steps of faith.

STRENGTH THROUGH SCRIPTURE

- **2 Corinthians 12:10** "I take pleasure in needs...For when I am weak, then I am strong."
- **Zechariah 4:6** "'Not by might nor by power, but by My Spirit,' says the LORD of hosts."
- **1 John 4:18** "There is no fear in love; but perfect love casts out fear."

PRACTICAL WISDOM

1. *Feed on testimonies and be aware of His love* – Review situations in your life and in the lives of others in which there was victory over a specific challenge. As you remember how God came through to bring victory in past situations, it will teach or remind you that His love for you will cast out all fear from you. When you become aware of His faithfulness and love in the past, your trust in Him will increase in the present. Rejoice and celebrate in His past faithfulness, and take pleasure in the fact that when we are weak, then He is strong.

2. *Pursue people who have been victorious in similar situations* – It is not a sign of weakness or being unspiritual to find others to mentor us. God created us to be part of His body, and He loves it when we work and grow together. Be intentional about pursuing others who have had to trust God in similar situations, and learn from their experience.

3. *Take small steps* – Sometimes tackling a big task can be daunting but we can break it into smaller tasks that are much less intimidating. Take small steps, and make sure to celebrate every accomplished task, no matter how small it is! Thank Him for helping you accomplish every little task and for walking right by your side throughout the whole thing.

DECLARATIONS

- God always shows up when I feel scared or insecure.
- God has prepared the way before me and is putting strategic people in my path to help me along the way.
- Every time I step out in faith, I grow in my awareness of God's love.

21 YOU LOOK IN THE MIRROR, AND YOU THINK YOU LOOK UGLY

CRUCIAL MOMENT

Ugh! You look at yourself in the mirror and have that sinking feeling again. You notice all your flaws. You've tried this and tried that to improve your looks, but nothing seems to be helping. You think about people you know who seem to always look good, and you get more depressed. You wonder if you can ever be really successful or happy because of the way your body appears. You are afraid that if you don't see something different in the mirror, then you will never be something different. In this moment, you know you have a choice to make.

WHAT TO GET EXCITED ABOUT

- You get to learn how to celebrate and love yourself when you are not perfect.

- You have the opportunity to find victory in this area, and share it with many others who struggle with negative feelings about their looks.

- This is a chance to get to triumph in the revelation that we are spirit beings who have a body. While our body is what we live in, it does not determine our identity or value.

STRENGTH THROUGH SCRIPTURE

- **Mark 12:31** "You shall love your neighbor as yourself . . ."

- **1 Peter 3:3-4** "Do not let your adornment be merely outward—arranging the hair, wearing gold, or putting on fine apparel— rather let it be the hidden person of the heart, with the incorruptible beauty of a gentle and quiet spirit, which is very precious in the sight of God."

- **1 Corinthians 13:4-7** "Love suffers long and is kind; love does not envy; love does not parade itself, is not puffed up; does not behave rudely, does not seek its own, is not provoked, thinks no evil; does not rejoice in iniquity, but rejoices in the truth; bears all things, believes all things, hopes all things, endures all things."

PRACTICAL WISDOM

1. *Understand the nature of the battle we are in* – Every person alive has things they wish were different about their looks. This dissatisfaction is fueled by advertisements of airbrushed models whose "perfection" strongly tempts us to feel less than adequate in our appearance. The teasing and ridicule many receive during childhood also contributes to these negative identity beliefs. Certainly some will battle unhealthy beliefs more than others concerning their appearance, but we all will need to create an identity based on a healthy relationship with God, not from our appearance. Bless your body every day. You can say something like this, "I bless my body to be a fat-burning machine."

2. *Overcome the trap of constantly comparing yourself with others* – Comparing ourselves to others is usually not a productive step to take for healthy living. It is either going to lead to a feeling of pride and superiority, or it will take us down the path of feelings of being a failure. One helpful step to take when an attitude of comparison kicks in is to immediately start praying blessing over the one you are tempted to compare yourself with. This act will remove any ugliness in your spirit, which will create beauty on the inside that will soon shine out to others.

3. *Move forward in your life* – "And the Lord said to Moses, 'Why do you cry to Me? Tell the children of Israel to go forward'" (Exodus 14:15). When the Israelites moved forward, the Red Sea parted. Something dynamic will happen in our lives too when we are advancing. One of the greatest questions we can ask God is "What does it look like for me to move forward in my life?" People who are progressing in life will face much less emotional trauma than those who are stagnant.

DECLARATIONS

- God always shows up when I look in the mirror and think I look ugly.

- I am beautiful, and I love being me.

- My internal beauty radiates through my face to others. I have a unique ability to resolve disagreements in my relationships.

22

SOMEONE IN YOUR LIFE JUDGES YOUR HEART AND MOTIVES UNFAIRLY

CRUCIAL MOMENT

As humans, we tend to judge ourselves by our motives and others by their actions. Too many times, there are miscommunications and unnecessary disconnects as a result of people making assumptions about one another. During these times, feelings of anger, frustration, sadness, and even rejection can creep in and try to make you feel like their judgment about you is your identity. Though these situations do not feel good, they do provide crucial moments for you to believe differently about the situation.

WHAT TO GET EXCITED ABOUT

- You get to love those who persecute you.
- This is an opportunity to choose to "keep your love on" no matter what someone else does.
- This is a chance to look inside at some of the adjustments you could make in an area of your life that may be a blind spot.

STRENGTH THROUGH SCRIPTURE

- **Proverbs 25:21** "If your enemy is hungry give him bread to eat; and if he is thirsty give him water to drink."
- **Matthew 5:44** "But I say to you, love your enemies, bless those who persecute you..."
- **James 1:19-20** "So the, my beloved brethren, let every man be swift to hear, slow to speak, slow to wrath; for the wrath of man does not produce righteousness of God."

PRACTICAL WISDOM

1. *Invite feedback* – It is easy when you feel misjudged to get angry and gossip to others about the problem. Instead of going down this road, why not take the opportunity to invite feedback in this area from a trusted person in your life? We all have blind spots, and close friends can often walk us through these things without creating offense.

2. *Keep your love on* – The most common thing people do when they have been hurt is to disconnect completely from a relationship. You can put walls up and shut your heart down. It is difficult to live like that. By keeping your love turned on regardless of what someone else does, you communicate you are open to working this out, no matter how it feels. There are times where you will need to communicate with words to this person and let them know how it affected you. Whatever you choose to do, keeping your love on will help even in the middle of confrontation.

3. *Don't label people* – Once you put a label on someone, you make them your enemy. By making them your enemy, you give yourself permission to be shut-down in the relationship and even to gossip about them. This cannot happen if you are choosing to stay connected in a relationship. Instead, find creative methods to bless and encourage them in practical ways.

DECLARATIONS

- God always shows up when someone judges me unfairly.
- I am un-offendable and choose to love those who hurt or judge me.
- God gives me supernatural wisdom to know what to do when someone judges me unfairly.

CRUCIAL MOMENT

You are praying for a negative circumstance to change and absolutely nothing has happened. You've prayed much about it, had many scriptural promises highlighted to you about it, and numerous people have come up to you and given you a "word from God" saying breakthrough will happen soon. In your persistence and longing for breakthrough, you've even had big name preachers pray for you. Despite all your efforts, none of it seems to have helped. Decades have gone by and you are losing hope. After all this time, you get to decide if it is worth believing for breakthrough a little longer or giving up and moving on.

WHAT TO GET EXCITED ABOUT

- You get to learn how to walk in hope, joy, and love before you experience breakthrough.

- This is an opportunity to develop greater compassion for others with long-standing, unchanging situations.

- This is a chance to trust God and believe He is good, even when you don't understand.

STRENGTH THROUGH SCRIPTURE

- **John 5:5-9** "One of the men lying there had been sick for thirty-eight years . . . instantly the man was healed."

- **Luke 1:7-24** "But they had no child, because Elizabeth was barren, and they were both well advanced in years.. . . . Now after those days his wife Elizabeth conceived."

- **Luke 13:11-13** "There was a woman who had a spirit of infirmity eighteen years, and was bent over and could in no way raise herself up. But when Jesus saw her, He called her to Him and said to her, 'Woman, you are loosed from your infirmity.' And He laid His hands on her, and immediately she was made straight, and glorified God."

PRACTICAL WISDOM

1. *Recognize that the length of time a problem has existed does not determine the likelihood of breakthrough* – The Bible frequently shares the length of a person's situation before the miracle happened (i.e. thirty-eight years - the man by pool in John 5, twelve years - the woman with issue of blood in Mark 5, eighteen years - the woman with the spirit of infirmity in Luke 13, etc.). These biblical testimonies are a great encouragement to us as we consider any long-standing adversities in our lives.

2. *Trust in the Lord with all your heart, and lean not on your own understanding* – Many in the Bible had a deep work of the Spirit done in their lives while waiting for their promise to manifest. Abraham, Joseph, Moses, and others developed intimacy with God and strong character during seasons when it looked like their vision had died. They discovered the joy of loving the promise-giver more than the promise itself. Like them, our times of waiting are an opportunity to find God in incredible ways.

3. *Hear the proceeding word of the Lord* – Matthew 4:4 tells us we live "by every word that proceeds from the mouth of God." The quality of our lives depends on our identifying what God has said. Indeed we are to "war a good warfare" (1 Timothy 1:18) with what has been spoken to us. As we face long-standing issues, there will be times when we are to diligently revisit scriptural promises and clarify what has been spoken to us. This gives an opportunity to hear a fresh heavenly word or new divine strategy to cause life to manifest in the area which has been dead for a long time.

DECLARATIONS

- God always shows up when I am battling a long-standing issue.

- I have an unusual ability to bring breakthrough to problems that have lasted a decade or longer.

- Like Abraham, my hope and faith increase the longer an unfulfilled promise exists.

CRUCIAL MOMENT

Upon entering a meeting, you realize that you did not complete your portion of the presentation in time. You begin to panic as you sit down in front of your boss and realize you cannot make a habit of this behavior. You are not alone; people miss deadlines for many reasons. Sometimes a lack of planning is the cause, while other times laziness is the culprit. When you miss a deadline, the implications can be significant. You may get a demotion or even lose your job, but missing a deadline is an opportunity to see what is really inside of you. Sometimes the situation is out of your control, but in most cases a missed deadline can be an opportunity to go higher in your personal and work life.

WHAT TO GET EXCITED ABOUT

- You get to celebrate progress and not perfection in your life.
- This is an opportunity to see that others have grace for you in moments of weakness.
- This is a chance to expose and repair any cracks in your life management.

STRENGTH THROUGH SCRIPTURE

- **2 Corinthians 12:9** "And He said to me, 'My grace is sufficient for you, for My strength is made perfect in weakness.'"
- **Proverbs 16:3** "Commit your works to the Lord and your thoughts will be established."
- **Proverbs 21:25** "The desire of a lazy man kills him, for his hands refuse to labor."

PRACTICAL WISDOM

1. *Create a project timeline* – For many people, working on several projects at a time is common. While making a daily to-do list is a good idea, it can be helpful to think more long-term. At the beginning of a project, create a timeline of goals and deadlines. This will help you to see the big picture in incremental steps. It can be intimidating to take on a big project, so breaking it down into smaller goals with deadlines for each will set you up for success. Create reminders on your calendar, computer, or smart-phone for extra support.

2. *Review daily goals the night before* – Once you have your goals mapped out with benchmarks and deadlines, you need a way to keep the process at the forefront of your mind. Developing a system of reviewing tomorrow's goals the night before can help keep you on track in all the areas of your life. Not only will it help you keep your deadlines, it will give practical time to think about what else is going on in your life. Utilizing this strategy will help you remember doctor's appointments, meetings, and other important events. Try setting S.M.A.R.T. goals. The acronym SMART stands for Specific, Measurable, Attainable, Realistic, and Time-sensitive. This model for goal-setting helps people grasp the important elements involved in reaching goals successfully.

3. *Believe you can do it* - There are hundreds of research findings that correlate a lack of success with a lack of belief. If we don't believe we are capable of doing something, we will not be able to do it more than a few times. If you find yourself missing many deadlines, assess your beliefs and mindsets in this area. You cannot consistently do what you don't believe you are, so it might require you to change the way you believe in order to see success.

DECLARATIONS

- God always shows up when I miss my deadline.
- I set specific, measurable, attainable, realistic, and time-sensitive goals.
- I meet all my deadlines with excellence and accuracy.

CRUCIAL MOMENT

You are so blessed to be a part of Overflowing Network of Ministries and have found new richness in your life as a result of its powerful nature. You particularly admire the group's main leader. He is a charismatic, influential leader recognized by many in the body of Christ as a voice of power and wisdom. Your adoration for this leader turns to shock when you hear he has been having an affair. You are hurt and confused, and you wonder if you can ever trust a leader again.

WHAT TO GET EXCITED ABOUT

- You get to reaffirm that your trust is not in man, but in God.

- You have the opportunity to help restore this leader through your prayers and potentially in other ways.

- This is a chance to increase your influence to help leaders walk in wholeness and integrity.

STRENGTH THROUGH SCRIPTURE

- **Proverbs 3:5-6** "Trust in the Lord with all your heart, and lean not on your own understanding; in all your ways acknowledge Him, and He shall direct your paths."

- **Galatians 6:1** "Brethren, if a man is overtaken in any trespass, you who are spiritual restore such a one in a spirit of gentleness, considering yourself lest you also be tempted."

- **Romans 8:28** "And we know that all things work together for good to those who love God, to those who are the called according to His purpose."

PRACTICAL WISDOM

1. ***Purpose to walk with God no matter what others do*** – Say this: "My faith and walk with Jesus do not depend on what others do." This commitment will be tested when someone we highly respect disappoints us through making horrible choices. Even so, those moments of leadership scandals give us an opportunity to further eliminate any unhealthy dependence we have on the influencers in our lives.

2. ***Develop your skills to restore others*** – Scripture says spiritual people have the ability to restore those "overtaken in any trespass" (Galatians 6:1). Whether we are helping someone very close to us or implementing restorative attitudes and actions from a distance, it is wise for us to have already strengthened our restorative skills before a crisis hits. This skillset includes compassion, prayer, wisdom, confrontation, ministering to root causes of the problem, developing plans to move forward, and helping those affected by sin. Decide what action step is best based on your relationship to the person.

3. ***Commit yourself to become an influencer of leaders*** – It is easy to be a critic in the grandstands of life about those who step forward to lead, but it takes maturity and intentionality to build trust in the eyes of leaders so you can become a positive influence to them. Here are six suggestions to build healthy relationships with leaders: 1) Avoid having a personal agenda except to be a blessing to them. 2) Pray for them. 3) Respect their boundaries in relationships. 4) Be specifically thankful to them. 5) Learn how to express concerns without attacking them. 6) Live a life of consistency, integrity, and spiritual advancement.

DECLARATIONS

- God always shows up when a church leader I respect has a moral failure.

- I have powerful and healthy relationships with leaders.

- I have an incredible ability to bring restoration to those who have fallen into sin.

26 YOU WALK INTO A ROOM FULL OF STRANGERS AND FEEL OUT OF PLACE

CRUCIAL MOMENT

All afternoon you have been thinking about the party you got invited to later that evening. The hours fly by, and you find yourself standing on the porch trying to get the courage to knock on the door. You are not afraid of people, but you are keenly aware that of the fifty people on the other side of that door, you know only one. You want people to feel valued by you and loved, but the fear of awkward conversations, small talk, and standing in the corner alone with your drink are plaguing your mind. You make a decision to take the next step. As you walk into the room, you cannot find your one friend anywhere. It is in this moment that you have a choice to make. You can stand in the corner and give life to your fears, or you can destroy them by engaging the room with confidence. The decision is a big one and only you can make it.

WHAT TO GET EXCITED ABOUT

- You get to see that you are likeable and people want to be around you.
- You have an opportunity to face the fear of rejection head on.
- This is a chance to make new, meaningful relationships.

STRENGTH THROUGH SCRIPTURE

- **2 Timothy 1:7** "For God has not given us a spirit of fear, but of power and of love and of a sound mind."
- **1 Peter 2:17** "Honor all people. Love the brotherhood. Fear God. . ."
- **2 Corinthians 13:11** "Finally, brethren, farewell. Become complete. Be of good comfort, be of one mind, live in peace; and the God of love and peace will be with you."

PRACTICAL WISDOM

1. *Overcome fear by imagining success* – The emotion of fear can be powerful and keep you from the very things that will be meaningful in your life. The enemy likes to replay all your failures and mistakes over and over again in your mind. When you entertain these thoughts long enough, he doesn't have to help you reminisce about your mistakes anymore because you inherently begin to expect the worst all on your own. Instead of giving in to this, try imagining what it would look like to be successful in this situation. Instead of picturing yourself wallowing in a corner, try imagining yourself having a productive and life-giving conversation with someone you decided to introduce yourself to. You will bring courage to yourself and overcome fear.

2. *Dress for success* – Often, the first insecurity you experience in a new group of people is related to what you look like. While your physical appearance is no sign of your value or worth, it will communicate certain messages to those around you and is the first thing people see. You get to determine what it looks like for you to "dress for success." Success is a state of being that starts on the inside. Make declarations, find your favorite shirt, or wear the perfume that everyone always comments on. Little things can make a big difference. Find what works for you, and it will boost your confidence in these new situations.

3. *Pre-plan conversation starters* – Not everyone can walk into a room of strangers and feel comfortable walking up to someone they do not know to start a conversation. If you have never called yourself a social butterfly, maybe now is the time to start. Before you go to the party, make a list of things you would like to know about someone and practice asking it in the mirror. This might seem silly, but it will help you in the moment of anxiety because you have already done it ahead of time.

DECLARATIONS

*   God always shows up when I walk into a room full of strangers.
*   I am self-confident and good at starting conversations with new people.
*   When I walk into a room of strangers, everyone wants to get to know me.

27 AN INCREDIBLE OPPORTUNITY ARISES AT A LESS THAN OPPORTUNE TIME

CRUCIAL MOMENT

Someone makes you an offer about something you've dreamed of for years. However, there are many reasons now making it a less than brilliant offer to accept. Maybe accepting it would force you to break another commitment. Perhaps the offer comes during an extremely inconvenient season for your spouse or family. For whatever reason, it just doesn't seem like the "right time," but still you're finding it hard to reject the amazing opportunity.

WHAT TO GET EXCITED ABOUT

- You get to steward this opportunity well, whether or not this is the right time. The fact that it is before you is evidence of favor.

- This is an opportunity to grow your relationship with God. This is a time where you and God get to grow closer. He's not going to leave you.

- This is a chance to learn to separate anxiety, fear, and lies from truth and love in a very practical way. There is hope!

STRENGTH THROUGH SCRIPTURE

- **Proverbs 2:6** "For the Lord gives wisdom; from His mouth come knowledge and understanding."

- **Proverbs 22:29 & 23:1-3** "Do you see a man who excels in his work? He will stand before kings; he will not stand before unknown men. When you sit down to eat with a ruler, consider carefully what is before you; and put a knife to your throat if you are a man given to appetite. Do not desire his delicacies, for they are deceptive food." (Considering these four verses, are you ready to "dine with kings"? Which man or woman are you currently?)

PRACTICAL WISDOM

1. *Opportunities, like money and talents, must be stewarded well* – The parable of the talents is a good starting point here (Matthew 25:14-30). You have an opportunity to steward favor and be aware of the lasting impact. Are you ready to steward now, or should you decline the offer so you can focus on growing your weaker points and strengthening your beliefs to a level equal to your apparent favor?

2. *Chase out fear* – It might be easy in this time to panic and believe lies such as, "If I don't accept this opportunity, I might never get another one like it!" (Let's just laugh at that, by the way.) Then again, if fear is keeping you where you are and away from the opportunity, that's the enemy's plan too. Chase out the fear and find your truth by sitting still in a quiet place with God. Slather Him with praise and thanksgiving, and listen to what the Holy Spirit says to you. Where is your peace in this decision?

3. *Ask good questions* – It's important not to just go with your initial feelings. Ask good questions of God, yourself, those that will be affected by your decision (such as your spouse), and those opening the door of opportunity to you. You may find that there are blended options, or that you've assumed things that aren't true or as rigid as they actually are.

DECLARATIONS

- God always shows up when I have favor and want to use it to glorify Him.
- I am powerful because I live full of hope and absent of fear.
- God has an EPIC plan for my life, and there's absolutely no way I'm going to miss out on it.

CRUCIAL MOMENT

You've had a long term physical issue and received prayer for it on multiple occasions over the years. When it comes to mind you often think of past experiences when you pursued God's intervention (asked for prayer, responded to a word of knowledge, etc.) and "nothing happened." Renewing your mind with these past disappointments has built a negative expectation in you, making receiving prayer difficult. You're visiting your friend's church and after preaching, the pastor asks anyone needing healing to come forward for prayer. Your heart sinks as you face a decision - will you hope again?

WHAT TO GET EXCITED ABOUT

- You get to know that every time someone prays something happens whether it manifests physically or not.

- You have the opportunity to believe God's promises in the face of opposing circumstances– which is an opportunity you will never get in heaven.

- This is a chance to realize that the bigger the resistance you face, the greater your story of God's intervention will be.

STRENGTH THROUGH SCRIPTURE

- **Psalm 103:2-3** "Praise the Lord, my soul, and forget not all his benefits— who forgives all your sins and heals all your diseases."

- **2 Chronicles 16:12** (NIV) "...Asa was afflicted with a disease in his feet. Though his disease was severe, even in his illness he did not seek help from the Lord, but only from the physicians."

- **John 5:5-9** "Now a certain man was there who had an infirmity thirty-eight years. When Jesus saw him lying there, and knew that he already had been in that condition a long time, He said to him, 'Do you want to be made well?' . . . 'Rise, take up your bed and walk.' And immediately the man was made well."

PRACTICAL WISDOM

1. *Refuse to limit God by the time-frame attached to your issue* - Scripture often reports the time-span of unresolved issues to teach us that the longevity of our issue does not hinder God's ability to bring restoration or healing. Determine in your heart to not limit God by the time frame attached to the issue.

2. *Determine that your beliefs will not be dictated by your experience but by God's Word* - Often when our experience doesn't line up with what God's Word says to be true, we adjust truth to make ourselves more comfortable with our circumstances. This response can lead to creating doctrines such as "It's not God's will to heal everyone," or "God sometimes allows sickness to remain in order to teach people character." Protect yourself from doctrines rooted in disappointment. Choose to embrace the mystery of the moment, believing God's promises in the face of negative circumstances.

3. *Trust in the Lord with all your heart and lean not on your own understanding (Proverbs 3:5-6)* - Sometimes things happen that are not easily explained. If our trust in God is based in our understanding, it will be difficult to trust Him when our circumstances are not logical. Learn to trust God from your heart by taking time to connect with Him and stirring your heart toward Him. As a wise man once said, the mind makes a great slave but a terrible master. Learn to lead your mind with your heart.

DECLARATIONS

- God always shows up when I receive prayer again for something which has been unchanging in my life.

- My faith is not dependent upon what I see, feel, or experience, but it is dependent on God's Word.

- I get healed more easily than anyone I know.

29 YOU SEE SOMEONE WITH A SIGN ASKING FOR MONEY

CRUCIAL MOMENT

You go to the grocery store to stock up for the week. As you walk in, next to the door is someone holding a sign saying, "Will work for food." Your heart fills with compassion for them, but you also wonder if he might be using the money for drugs or alcohol. You want to give him something, but you are unsure. You fight the conflicting feelings inside you and are left with a decision to make.

WHAT TO GET EXCITED ABOUT

- You get to recommit in your heart that you are a person who gives to the poor.
- You have the opportunity to become a powerful decision-maker who decides out of faith, not Christian obligation.
- This is a chance to connect with Holy Spirit on what you are to do.

STRENGTH THROUGH SCRIPTURE

- **Matthew 25:40** "Assuredly, I say to you, inasmuch as you did it to one of the least of these My brethren, you did it to Me."
- **2 Thessalonians 3:10** "For even when we were with you, we commanded you this: If anyone will not work, neither shall he eat."
- **Genesis 41:35-36** "And let them gather all the food of those good years that are coming . . . Then that food shall be as a reserve for the land for the seven years of famine which shall be in the land of Egypt, that the land may not perish during the famine."

PRACTICAL WISDOM

1. *Challenge yourself to grow in your generosity to the poor* – "For God so loved the world that He gave His only Son . . ." (John 3:16). God compassionately gave to a people who could not repay Him. We have the privilege of determining that we too will be givers. Something powerful happens when we develop a heart for the less-fortunate and decide to help them in finances, encouragement, and in other ways. This decision breaks off selfishness in us and causes us to be God's hand extended to others.

2. *Be spontaneous in giving, but focus more on planned giving* – It is one thing to give to a need presenting itself, but it is even more powerful to set money aside to proactively give. The tithe is an example of planned giving. As we give regularly to ministries and organizations which are helping the poor with their immediate needs and in developing the tools to overcome poverty, we will ultimately make a greater impact than only giving to people we come across. We can also become more proactive in our "spontaneous giving" by having "Holy Spirit fun money" with us to give as needs present themselves to us (or to give as Holy Spirit leads).

3. *Know there are times you won't give to immediate needs because of commitments you have already made to others* – Some give generously to people they don't know, and then have little or nothing left for their family and loved ones (or for fulfilling promises they've made of paying off debts or other financial commitments). This type of behavior sends the wrong message to the people closest to us, and it ultimately could be a character issue which will derail our influence and favor.

DECLARATIONS

- God always shows up when I see someone who is asking for money.
- I am very generous to the poor.
- I make great decisions in my giving, and I regularly support ministries who serve the poor.

SOMEONE GETS PROMOTED AHEAD OF YOU FOR A POSITION YOU FEEL YOU DESERVED

CRUCIAL MOMENT

You work really hard. Every single day of your work life, you go the extra mile, do more than expected, and troubleshoot problems before they happen. You, and everyone else in your company, know that you are in line for the next promotion. Excitement fills your heart when the promotion is announced as you have been waiting for this moment for a while. Unexpectedly, your boss calls the name of someone who you feel has not performed as well as you. This is a crucial moment for you to consider how to posture yourself and celebrate someone else's promotion.

WHAT TO GET EXCITED ABOUT

- You get to celebrate another person, regardless of whether or not you think they deserve what they have received.
- This is an opportunity to practice being successful on the inside when you are not seemingly successful on the outside.
- This is a chance to discern the times and seasons of favor for you and for others.

STRENGTH THROUGH SCRIPTURE

- **Colossians 3:23-24** "And whatever you do, do it heartily, as to the Lord and not to men, knowing that from the Lord you will receive the reward of the inheritance; for you serve the Lord Christ."
- **1 Chronicles 12:32** "...of the sons of Issachar who had understanding of the times, to know what Israel ought to do"
- **Ecclesiastes 3:1** "To everything there is a season, a time for every purpose under heaven"

PRACTICAL WISDOM

1. *Celebrate the promotion with something thoughtful* – It would be very easy to list all the reasons why you believe you deserved that promotion and to withhold celebration. Instead, this is a great opportunity to celebrate the person in a practical way. Write them a card, buy them a small gift, send flowers, or find a way to express genuine celebration. The celebration of others will take your eyes off of you and disarm the spirit of entitlement.

2. *Resolve not to promote yourself* - Let God promote you in due time, trusting that He is your biggest fan, your Advocate, and Friend. If you honor and promote yourself, you will find yourself working to maintain the promotion from your own strength and energy. On the other hand, when God promotes you, He always provides the grace (divine enablement) for you to thrive and succeed from your new platform of favor.

3. *Intentionally steward the season you are in and be open to adjustments you need to make in your life* – It is easy to miss what God is doing in a season like this because we focus on what we are not receiving. This season is a process designed to prepare you for what is to come. Spend time with God asking Him to teach you how to discern times and seasons. Additionally, ask for strategies to implement now to benefit you in your season of promotion. Focus on what you are becoming through now. It might be a good idea to take a personal inventory and look for blind spots that hinder promotion. If you find some, make small adjustments accordingly.

DECLARATIONS

- God always shows up when someone gets promoted ahead of me.
- I celebrate the promotions of people in my life as testimonies of God's goodness.
- I discern times and seasons of favor well.

31   AN INCESSANT TALKER IS APPROACHING YOU

CRUCIAL MOMENT

You are getting ready to leave a gathering when you see an incessant talker coming toward you. Your heart sinks. Your mind races through previous situations where you have been stuck listening to his verbal marathons of talking endlessly about his life and what he thinks about everything under the sun. You try to avoid eye contact with him as you head toward the door, but he cuts you off and says, "I am so glad to see you! I felt the Lord wanted me to tell you my new revelation about the atomic particles in the wood of Noah's ark." You smile, but inwardly you are saying, "No! Not again!" Much like a fight or flight decision, you have a choice to make a powerful decision about what you are going to do.

WHAT TO GET EXCITED ABOUT

- You get to learn how to love people at higher levels.

- You have the opportunity to develop greater capacity to live a life that is not controlled by others.

- This is a chance to learn how to help others become more successful in their relationships.

STRENGTH THROUGH SCRIPTURE

- **Ephesians 4:15** "Speaking the truth in love . . ."

- **1 Corinthians 13:5-7** "[Love] does not behave rudely, does not seek its own, is not provoked, thinks no evil . . . bears all things, believes all things, hopes all things, endures all things."

- **Matthew 7:5** "First remove the plank from your own eye, and then you will see clearly to remove the speck from your brother's eye."

PRACTICAL WISDOM

1. *Receive a fresh measure of God's unconditional love to give away to others–* It is good to meditate on 1 Corinthians 13. We are told we can do great spiritual things, but they are of no value if we don't have love. The love mentioned in this chapter primarily concerns our attitudes in relationships. We are called to release the unconditional love we have received to those in our lives. As we receive God's love in our imperfection, then we are able to love and have compassion with others in their weakness.

2. *Learn skills to extract yourself from lengthy conversations* – Here are some ideas: 1) Jump into the conversation and interrupt the person to ask a question or make a comment so both of you are talking and you get a chance to have input. 2) Inform him of your time constraints: "I only have a few minutes." 3) Give options for future communication: "It is clear I am not going to be able to finish this conversation. Could you email me the rest or make an appointment with me?" 4) Have others help- You can develop some sort of signal (like pulling your ear) to alert key people to help get you out of such conversations.

3. *Help this person see the bigger picture* – Ultimately, someone who monopolizes the time of others needs to become aware of what is happening and how this is affecting his or her relationships. If it is a repeated happening with someone, find a time to share your heart by saying something like this. *"I so appreciate your heart to connect with me and share what is happening in your life. You may at times sense I am trying to pull away from these conversations. I want to explain why I do this."* And then share your heart. Let them know what you can and cannot do. Give them options of what to do.

DECLARATIONS

*   God always shows up when an incessant talker approaches me.

*   I am very successful in the conversations I have with a wide variety of people.

*   I greatly help others become blessed in how they interact in relationships.

32 THE UNTHINKABLE HAPPENS, AND YOU FEEL OUT OF CONTROL

CRUCIAL MOMENT

It's a regular day, and the phone rings. You answer, and the voice on the other end tells you something that makes your heart sink. Maybe the one you love has been unfaithful. Maybe your child has run away. Maybe your spouse lost their job. Although you would never desire this situation to happen, you still have a choice to be hopeful or hopeless. These crucial moments are some of the most important for us to bring God in and let Him do His thing, as well as find out what our role is to be in the solution.

WHAT TO GET EXCITED ABOUT

- You get avoid powerlessness and choose to be powerful in the situation.
- You have the opportunity to live out your faith to those in your life who have yet to meet Jesus.
- This is a chance to co-labor with Jesus, finding where your role ends and His begins. You're about to have a new testimony.

STRENGTH THROUGH SCRIPTURE

- **Psalm 46:10** "Be still, and know that I am God."
- **Romans 8:28** "And we know that all things work together for good to those who love God, to those who are the called according to His purpose.
- **1 John 4:18** "There is no fear in love; but perfect love casts out fear, because fear involves torment. But he who fears has not been made perfect in love."

PRACTICAL WISDOM

1. *Soak in God's Presence* – Be still before God until you have His perspective on the situation- until you feel His love for you. Though He hurts when you hurt, He is not hopeless about the situation. Find peace.

2. *Find your role* – Once you have God's perspective of peace and hope on the issue, ask Him for wisdom about what you are to do to help in the situation. There may be others who are suffering because of the situation, just as you are. Maybe they are having difficulty understanding how a good God could "let this happen." Look at what God is doing in you and in those around you and release peace to all those involved.

3. *Speak declarations of victory into the situation* – You may not feel like doing so, but speaking declarations of God's promises is a key step for breakthrough to occur. Not only does making declarations cause a shift in the situation, limiting the access of the enemy who wants to cause greater harm, but it keeps us looking for and expecting God to show up.

DECLARATIONS

- God always shows up when the unthinkable happens and turns it to good.
- I am incredibly blessed and highly favored. God's grace is sufficient for me to make it through this situation in victory.
- God is good all the time. He will turn this situation around for good in my life and the lives impacted by it.

33 YOU DON'T FEEL VALUED

CRUCIAL MOMENT

You feel manipulated, used, dishonored, or ignored by a boss, spouse, or friend. We are all called to serve and honor others, but sometimes it can get tricky when the person we're serving doesn't respect or honor us in return. Moments like these are filled with options. Do we keep serving? Do we put up walls around our hearts? Do we act like nothing's wrong? At times like these, insecurities, wrong attitudes, and bitterness can slip in without us even realizing it. We can let our heart go with the flow and be led by emotions or we can make a decision and tell our heart how to respond. What are we going to do?

WHAT TO GET EXCITED ABOUT

- You get to receive insight from God in order to understand the person you're serving and love them with His love.
- You have the opportunity to reaffirm where you are getting your value from and grow in your awareness of God's love towards you.
- This is a chance to live like someone who has been co-crucified with Christ and is free from needing man's approval.

STRENGTH THROUGH SCRIPTURE

- **Galatians 2:20** "I have been crucified with Christ; it is no longer I who live, but Christ lives in me; and the life which I now live in the flesh I live by faith in the Son of God, who loved me and gave Himself for me."
- **Ephesians 1:17** "That the God of our Lord Jesus Christ, the Father of glory, may give to you the spirit of wisdom and revelation in the knowledge of Him."
- **Luke 6:28** "Bless those who curse you, and pray for those who spitefully use you."

PRACTICAL WISDOM

1. *Remember who you are and don't partner with self-pity* – You are a new creation in Christ Jesus. You are a son or daughter of the Most High, and you have access to His presence. Remind yourself of these truths and fill up on the love of God. When we are full of His love, we no longer look for the love and acceptance of others to satisfy us. Refusing to partner with self-pity will also stop the enemy from poisoning you with a spirit of entitlement. Instead, as you fill up on the love of God, embrace a spirit of gratitude for who you are in Him.

2. *Put on God's lenses and pray for others* – Everyone goes through situations like these sooner or later, but as sons and daughters of God, we have the supernatural ability to see others like God does. Ask God for a heavenly perspective to view the people involved as God does, and believe for creative ways to pour out His love upon them. Start blessing and praying for the person who isn't valuing you. Go past just praying for the situation and bless their families, friends, and finances. Praying for others is an effective tool to keeping bitterness from creeping into our hearts.

3. *Ask for advice* – If you're facing a decision based on being mistreated or used, ask others for advice as to how to put up healthy boundaries while still loving and serving with a good attitude. They can also help you determine if you are to change the nature of your relationship with this person. Remember, God loves you as much as He loves the one you're serving, and He's big enough to send someone else to show His love to them if it's His time for you to go in a different direction.

DECLARATIONS

- God always shows up when I don't feel valued and lavishes His overflowing love and acceptance upon me.

- I am full of wisdom and insight to understand those I serve and to make great decisions.

- I am free from bitterness and am able to bless the lives, families, and finances of those that I serve.

34 YOU CAN'T GET MOTIVATED TO START THE DAY

CRUCIAL MOMENT

It's early, really early. The sound of your alarm is like nails on a chalkboard, but after hitting the snooze button a half dozen times, you realize you are going to be late if you don't get up. From the moment you get out of bed, everything goes wrong: your water is not working, your clothes are wrinkled, and when you look in the mirror, the face staring back at you looks tired, worn out, and not ready to face the day. On these days, you may be tempted to jump back in bed and pull the covers over your head to avoid facing the world, but these "tough" mornings present you with a crucial moment as to whether you will conquer the morning or the morning will conquer you!

WHAT TO GET EXCITED ABOUT

* You get to strengthen your beliefs about your own self-control.

* This is an opportunity to experience the truth that God's mercies are new every single day! A new day is a fresh start. You never get to start today over again.

* This is a chance to realize that even when circumstances are difficult, you are equipped to get breakthrough in the area of developing habits for a successful life.

STRENGTH THROUGH SCRIPTURE

* **Lamentations 3:22-23** "Through the Lord's mercies we are not consumed, because His compassions fail not. They are new every morning; great is Your faithfulness."

* **Numbers 13:30** "Then Caleb quieted the people before Moses, and said, 'Let us go up at once and take possession, for we are well able to overcome it.'"

* **Psalm 66:20** "Blessed be God, who has not turned away my prayers, nor His mercy from me."

PRACTICAL WISDOM

1. *Refuse to hit the snooze button* – Have you ever heard the phrase, "You snooze; you lose"? Well, if you are hitting the snooze button, this could be true. Experts agree that hitting the snooze button is one of the worst things you can do when you start your morning. An hour before your internal clock sets to wake you up, your body prepares to rise. When you hit the snooze button, you transition back to deep sleep causing you to be groggy and disturbing your body's chemistry. Instead of hitting the snooze button, try setting the alarm for the exact time you need to get up, or place your alarm clock across the room, requiring you to get out of bed to turn it off.

2. *Attack the morning . . . Before morning* – Making a plan the night before about what your morning will look like will help you feel more in control in the crucial moments just after the alarm goes off. For most people, having a plan leads to success in stressful and difficult situations. This could look like waking up to time with the Lord or going to the gym, but no matter what you do, giving yourself something to look forward to will help you attack the morning instead of the morning attacking you.

3. *Refuse to make excuses* – One of the easiest things to do in the mornings is compromise. You may have said to yourself or others, "Well, I am just not a morning person." Making this declaration perpetuates the problem and often leads to unsuccessful mornings. On the other hand, you can refuse to compromise your sleep by going to bed at a good hour and getting up when your alarm goes off. This will make you more successful in other areas of life as well.

DECLARATIONS

- God always shows up when my alarm goes off and I don't want to get up.
- God's mercies are new every day and that includes mornings.
- I am a morning person.

35 YOU ARE MOCKED WHILE SHARING THE GOSPEL

CRUCIAL MOMENT

You notice an elderly man sitting at a bus stop in front of you. He looks friendly, and you think to yourself, "I'm going to tell this guy about Jesus." You walk up to him. "Excuse me sir, I've got some good news for you…" Instantly, the man's countenance changes as he snaps, "Oh no! You're not one of those Jesus freaks are you? I've had enough!" Cursing God, his once gentle face transfigures, "How can you believe that garbage!?" You stand there stunned as he doesn't back down but keeps screaming in your face. "You are ill-informed! You're doing nothing but playing mind-games with people. All you Christians are the same! How do you explain Noah's Ark!?" Suddenly you realize that bystanders are noticing the screaming man and are stopping to watch. You see a couple neighborhood boys laughing hysterically, "The Jesus man is getting it from Grandpa!"

WHAT TO GET EXCITED ABOUT

- You get to discover greater depths of the supernatural love and peace of God.
- You have the opportunity to love someone who is obviously hurting, probably because of some bad past experiences.
- This is a chance to overcome any hint of the fear of man that may surface in your heart during this special moment.

STRENGTH THROUGH SCRIPTURE

- **1 John 4:16,18** "He who abides in love abides in God, and God in him… There is no fear in love; but perfect love casts out fear."
- **Galatians 2:20** "I have been crucified with Christ; it is no longer I who live, but Christ lives in me."
- **Matthew 5:10-12** "Blessed are those who are persecuted for righteousness' sake, for theirs is the kingdom of heaven. Blessed are you when they revile and persecute you, and say all kinds of evil against you falsely for My sake. Rejoice and be exceedingly glad, for great is your reward in heaven."

PRACTICAL WISDOM

1. *Look for what is right with the person instead of what is wrong* - It is usually very easy to see faults in people – especially in situations like this! Look for and ask God to reveal to you the "gold" inside the person attacking you. Look past their "dirt" and uncover the dreams and desires God has put in their heart. Every person on the planet is made in the image of God, whether they know it or not. Simply honoring someone who dishonors you can often silence arguments and subdue anger.

2. *Always choose love* - People who respond in a dynamically negative way can be the closest to encountering God in a dynamically positive way. God isn't threatened by their rejection; He loves them. Don't forget that Jesus was a friend of sinners and He loved the world even while it nailed Him to a cross. Find creative ways to love the person in front of you, imploring them to be reconciled to God. Ask questions. Listen. Try giving a compliment. People will sometimes resist love for a while but no one can resist love forever.

3. *Determine to be a God Pleaser not a People Pleaser* - Sometimes it's OK to simply walk away when someone is mistreating you. Sow seeds of love and pray for them in private, but don't be surprised when people treat you with contempt as a follower of Christ. Be OK with not everyone liking you. Jesus was the most loving person to ever walk the planet, yet some deeply despised Him. If you are feeling frazzled by the rejection of people, take advantage of this exciting opportunity to grow in a deeper level of security in your identity as God's child.

DECLARATIONS

- God always shows up when people mock or ridicule me because of my faith.

- I am a bold witness of Christ's resurrection power.

- I love people well and always honor and bless others regardless of their actions or words.

70

CRUCIAL MOMENT

Businesses across the planet are attempting to find ways to maximize productivity; unfortunately, they are also doing their best to minimize costs. One of the ways of cutting costs is by creating over-crowded work environments. For anyone who has worked in a cubicle or a small space with no doors or separation from the rest of the office, you know it can be distracting. In an attempt to create more revenue, sometimes employees can get less work done because of conversation, visual distractions, or simple background noises. This scenario is a great opportunity to rise above a circumstance and find a way to be the most productive person in the office.

WHAT TO GET EXCITED ABOUT

- You get to be a thermostat determining the atmosphere in an environment.
- You have the opportunity to develop a greater level of patience and perseverance with difficult circumstances.
- This is a chance to practice brave communication with those in your office space.

STRENGTH THROUGH SCRIPTURE

- **Proverbs 16:3** "Commit your works to the Lord and your thoughts will be established."
- **Proverbs 9:9** "Give instruction to a wise man, and he will be still wiser; teach a just man, and he will increase in learning."
- **Hebrews 12:1** "Therefore we also, since we are surrounded by so great a cloud of witnesses, let us lay aside every weight, and the sin which so easily ensnares us, and let us run with endurance the race that is set before us."

PRACTICAL WISDOM

1. *Evaluate what you need in order to be productive* – It is easy to get caught up in what is going on around you while you are at work. Sometimes the distractions you experience are welcomed opportunities to procrastinate or not get your work done. This can be difficult at times, but it is important that you take time to evaluate what you need in order to be productive. Productivity and efficiency will almost always guarantee longevity in a job. Take an inventory of the common distractions you face and make a plan ahead of time for what you are going to do the next time it comes up.

2. *Communicate with those in your workspace what you are going to do* – You are not a victim of the people in your office. Though you may not like to cause controversy or stir the waters, it is important you learn to communicate what you are going to do. Next time a non-work-related discussion arises, let your co-workers know you will not participate this time. You can do this in a respectful way. Try saying, "It would really help me if you could wait until break time to have discussions not related to work as I have a lot to do. If your conversation is important, can you take it to another room?"

3. *Optimize your personal workspace* – There are a number of devices that can help you optimize your workspace. One of the best ways to remain distraction free in a high-traffic work area is to utilize noise-cancelling headphones. These will minimize noise even if no music is playing and help you focus on the task at hand. If your job does not allow headphones, create a system so people know you prefer to not be disturbed. One idea would be to incorporate a sign system that you can place for others to see when you are working and when you are open to questions and discussions. Even a simple, red, yellow, and green card can send a message without creating a problem.

DECLARATIONS

- God always shows up when my office environment is distracting.
- I am an excellent assessor of my needs.
- I am the most loving and honest communicator I know.

37 YOU GET YOUR FEELINGS HURT BY SOMEONE CLOSE TO YOU

CRUCIAL MOMENT

A close friend or family member has said or done something which was unexpected and hurtful to us. It has happened to all of us. Our emotions flare up – we may cry, have an angry outburst, dwell on the offense in silence, or we may speak negative things about the offender to others. These situations can be golden opportunities to grow radically in our relationships and emotional responses to being disappointed by others.

WHAT TO GET EXCITED ABOUT

- You get to grow in "keeping your love on" when relationships become challenging.

- You have the opportunity to overcome behaviors like anger, self-pity, and victimhood.

- This is a chance to learn how to strengthen your ability to process relationship trials in a healthy way.

STRENGTH THROUGH SCRIPTURE

- **Ephesians 4:32** "And be kind to one another, tenderhearted, forgiving one another, even as God in Christ forgave you."

- **Matthew 18:15** "If your brother sins against you, go and tell him his fault between you and him alone."

- **Matthew 7:5** "First remove the plank from your own eye, and then you will see clearly to remove the speck from your brother's eye."

PRACTICAL WISDOM

1. *Realize everyone will face some level of disappointment in your relationships* – The question is not "if" those closest to us will disappoint us, it is "when." We are connected with imperfect people who usually have differing expectations about the relationship. Overcoming disappointment in relationships is a key for successful living. This does not mean we allow ourselves to be abused or walked over by others, but it does mean we overcome the tendency of allowing the behavior of others to determine our joy and happiness in life.

2. *Practice the H.A.L.T. principle* – Never make a major decision or conclusion when you are hungry, angry, lonely, or tired. Understanding our situation (or what time of the month it is) will help protect us from trying to hurt those who have hurt us. This self-awareness will be important in our being able to focus on the truly important issues in the relationship, and it will also aid us in seeing clearly if there is a "plank" we need to remove from our eye before helping the behavior of another.

3. *Be a lifetime student of successful relationships and good communication* – The quality of our lives depends heavily upon our being successful in communication and in relationships. It is the wise person who proactively learns how to forgive, how to communicate expectations, how to listen well, how to set healthy boundaries, how and when to confront the negative behavior in others, and how to overcome any tendency to be easily offended.

DECLARATIONS

• God always shows up when I get my feelings hurt by someone close to me.

• I set healthy boundaries and am a great communicator in relationships.

• My deepest needs in life are met by God, not by another person.

38 THE ONE YOU LOVE DECIDES TO DISCONNECT AND PULL AWAY

CRUCIAL MOMENT

The one you love isn't exactly making you feel loved. Your "love tank" is dry, and your attempts at reconnection go nowhere. They don't seem to want to respond to anything that you say, and you're trying hard not to feel like a victim. You've got a big decision to make in how you handle this.

WHAT TO GET EXCITED ABOUT

- You get to see that the other person in the relationship is likely to be hurting. You get to respond in a way which is helpful in allowing God to touch them tenderly in that hurting place.

- This is an opportunity, like Jesus, to show love, despite your perception that you are not being loved in return.

- This is a chance to release the other person from the responsibility of how you feel inside and empower yourself to make decisions that affect your own internal peace and joy.

STRENGTH THROUGH SCRIPTURE

- **Ephesians 4:25** "Therefore, putting away lying, Let each one of you speak truth with his neighbor, for we are members of one another."

- **Proverbs 17:9** "He who covers a transgression seeks love, but he who repeats a matter separates friends."

- **Proverbs 10:19** "In the multitude of words sin is not lacking, but he who restrains his lips is wise."

PRACTICAL WISDOM

1. *Remember who they are* – This person likely wouldn't hurt you intentionally; so what's the issue? You have to remember who they are and step back, getting a new perspective. How have they interpreted the situation? How have they experienced you? They might be walking under the shadow of blame, or possibly under offense. Never forget who they are in God's eyes (the ultimate reality), and then address those things that are keeping you apart as separate issues from them as a person.

2. *Tell them how they affect you* – It's one thing to tell someone everything that they have done wrong. It's another thing to tell that person how what they did affected you. To you, one feels just as freeing as the other. But to them, they couldn't be more different. In the latter, you give them the information, and they get to decide how they want to respond. There's no hint of control or manipulation, unlike the accussatory first example.

3. *Take your time* – It is challenging not to react emotionally with angry accusations when we are hurt or offended. Think of it this way: if you are going to continue in relationship with this person, you're going to know them more and more in the future, and will be able to easily and patiently deal with the symptoms of their pain. So, take your time to feel love for that person before you react, love that you would immediately have if you knew more about them than you do now.

DECLARATIONS

- God always shows up when I have relationship problems.

- No one else is responsible for my internal peace and joy. I am in control of me.

- I am a good listener, a good speaker… a good communicator. I am a safe place.

39 YOUR COMPUTER CRASHES

CRUCIAL MOMENT

After a long train ride you finally arrive at work ready to start your day. You sit down at your workstation, pull out your laptop, and turn it on. Instead of the bright white light and two-tone noise that usually greets you at the beginning of your workday, you see a black screen that says "Internal Errors." What was once your worst nightmare has now become your reality. In the 21st Century, we depend on technology like we depend on air to breathe. Often, sensitive and very important information is stored on computers, smartphones, or electronic tablets, and simply the thought of it crashing causes major anxiety to come rushing in. A challenge of this magnitude is an opportunity to choose to rejoice in difficult situations.

WHAT TO GET EXCITED ABOUT

- You get to build greater problem-solving skills disasters happen with your electronic devices.
- You have the opportunity for an upgrade in your communication skills.
- This is a chance to build a proactive plan for protecting important information.

STRENGTH THROUGH SCRIPTURE

- **Romans 8:28** "All things work together for good for those who love God and are called according to His purposes."
- **Hebrews 10:23** "Let us hold fast the confession of our hope without wavering, for He who promised is faithful."
- **James 1:5** "If any of you lacks wisdom, let him ask of God, who gives to all liberally and without reproach, and it will be given to him."

PRACTICAL WISDOM

1. *Stay calm and hopeful* – When disastrous things happen in people's lives, the first response is usually to panic. Instead of panicking, try laughing and making declarations that all is not lost. Bringing hope to a seemingly hopeless situation is key to finding a favorable solution. One way to help do this is to make this declaration, "There is always a solution."

2. *Get professional help* – If you do not work at an office with an IT department, there are many places available for you to get IT help and recover what is lost. Computer crashes that cannot be repaired are very rare. A quick Internet search can find you information in your area to a qualified computer repair technician, or you can simply take it to a reputable electronic retail store for help.

3. *Be proactive* – It is a good practice to backup all your computer documents and files once a week at least. If you use your computer on a less frequent basis, then you could probably get by doing so every few weeks. There are cloud-based websites that can backup several gigabytes of information for free. This is an efficient, economical way to protect your information in the future and can be easily found by using a search function on any web browser.

DECLARATIONS

- God always shows up when my computer crashes.
- I am a great problem-solver when it comes to computer problems.
- I am proactive and efficient with the important details of my life.

40 YOU KEEP FORGETTING TO DO THINGS

CRUCIAL MOMENT

Ever had one of those days that seemed to be going as planned until you realized that you forgot something? You wake up, have an amazing time with God, head out to the office with a victorious mindset, but you realize you forgot to bring your computer to the office? Or you had an appointment with someone, and left them hanging? Or you forgot it was your anniversary? The natural response in situations like these is to want to kick yourself and be upset about how you "messed up," but you have a choice as to how you are going to react. What's it going to be?

WHAT TO GET EXCITED ABOUT

- You get to be surprised by God's provision as He uses the situation for good!

- You have the opportunity to grow in your ability to hear from the Holy Spirit as He gives you creative solutions.

- This is a chance to grow in your identity as the Father's son or daughter by choosing to see yourself the way He sees you, instead of seeing yourself as a forgetful disaster.

STRENGTH THROUGH SCRIPTURE

- **Romans 8:31** "What then shall we say to these things? If God is for us, who can be against us?"

- **2 Timothy 1:7** "For God has not given us a spirit of fear, but of power and of love and of a sound mind."

- **Romans 8:28** "And we know that all things work together for good to those who love God, to those who are the called according to His purpose."

PRACTICAL WISDOM

1. *Refuse to beat yourself up* – Many of us have been taught that if we feel bad enough, it will make us do better. That's not true! Studies show that getting upset with yourself increases stress hormones and inhibits creativity. It not only hinders you from being able to think of a creative solution to the problem, but it is also a way of partnering with the enemy and embracing lies such as "I'm a disaster!" or "I've messed everything up!" Instead, partner with what God thinks about you by refusing to get mad and frustrated with yourself when you fail and forget something.

2. *Remember God's greatness and choose to stay thankful* – We sometimes think that by forgetting something, we are messing up God's plans and creating problems that can't be solved – or we might think God is busy doing something more important, and suddenly He has to fix the "mess" that we created by forgetting something. But God is big enough to use our forgetfulness for good. As you remember that He delights in helping us and that our problems are never too complicated, burdensome, or untimely, refuse to fall into negativity and stay thankful. Focus on what God has already done and on how he's helping you solve the problem. When everything in you wants to get upset, beat yourself up, or worry, stop and think of what you can thank Him for.

3. *Get creative while taking practical steps to help you remember things* - If you tend to forget things on the way to work, then create a special place by the door where you always put those things before going to bed, if you forget to put those things in their special spot, then put an alarm on your phone that always goes off at night to remind you to put them in their special spot. Try to think of creative solutions to help you be less forgetful. Studies show that if you do something for 21 to 30 days, it will become a habit. Be patient with yourself as you create new habits and patterns of thinking.

DECLARATIONS

- God always shows up when I forget something and will always use whatever mistake I make for my good.

- God's plan for my life can't be messed up by my forgetfulness. Or: My forgetfulness can't mess up God's plan for my life.

- I am growing greatly in my ability to remember important things in my life.

41 SOMEONE ELSE GETS WHAT YOU'VE BEEN ASKING GOD FOR

CRUCIAL MOMENT

You've been asking God for a promotion, greater encounters in Him, and for a new car. You are fighting discouragement because nothing seems to be happening, yet others are receiving the very things that you've been asking for. At work, someone half your age (with less experience) gets promoted to the position you desire. In your church, a new convert testifies about an experience you have been asking God about for many years. And your neighbor is given a car, even though he has three already. As you consider these happenings and your feelings of discouragement, you suddenly realize . . . this is a crucial moment!

WHAT TO GET EXCITED ABOUT

- You get to learn how to steward God's blessing on someone else's life, knowing that this process is equipping you to properly steward your own blessings.

- You have the opportunity to observe your heart's response in a crucial moment of pressure, knowing that God is right there beside you. He is more than willing to pull any roots of jealousy or other noxious weeds which may be revealed.

- This is a chance to celebrate as if God just gave you the promotion, the encounter, or the car because every testimony of God is part of your heritage as a member of His family.

STRENGTH THROUGH SCRIPTURE

- **Luke 16:12** "And if you have not been faithful in what is another man's, who will give you what is your own?"

- **Psalm 84:11** "No good thing will He withhold from those who walk uprightly."

- **Psalm 119:111** "Your testimonies I have taken as a heritage forever, for they are the rejoicing of my heart."

PRACTICAL WISDOM

1. *Be honest about your feelings with God* - In moments like these, it is vital to tell God your true feelings. You may be experiencing jealousy, or even feeling like God doesn't love you. Jesus is looking for an honest heart; He wants to hear your feelings. When we ignore our feelings or live in denial, we bury a part of us inside, cutting ourselves off from Jesus' perspective in that area. Tell Jesus what's going on in your heart and invite His perspective. Don't miss this exciting opportunity for adjustment, healing, and growth.

2. *Make it a habit to instinctively celebrate God's favor on the lives of others*- When you are compelled to celebrate God's blessing on others' lives, it is an indication that you are living from a perspective of God's abundance. When not living from this perspective, getting what we want could in fact be detrimental to our spiritual health, reinforcing a bad belief that God is moved by our needs rather than faith in His radical goodness.

3. *Kill jealousy with kindness* - Guard yourself from jealousy, comparison, or a critical spirit by intentionally blessing people who experience God's favor in areas you are seeking God for. Investing into what God invests in helps recalibrate your heart to Heaven's perspective. Pray for that person you envy, congratulate them, or even invest into them financially. You'll find that not only will your attitude towards them change, but you'll also become a more likely recipient of God's blessings in your own life.

DECLARATIONS

- When others are blessed, I instinctively rejoice – especially when they are blessed with things I desire.

- God always shows up when others get things I've been asking for.

- I am a magnet for God's blessings; He loves to fulfill my desires.

CRUCIAL MOMENT

No matter what you have tried, you cannot find sleep. Knowing you have a long day tomorrow, you toss and turn, hoping to find that perfect position that will take you to dreamland. Like all the nights before, you see the clock turn with each passing hour as the sky becomes illuminated by morning. You roll out of bed, exhausted, and drag yourself through the day. Something has to change. If you face anymore nights like this, you don't think you are going to be able to function at all. This lack of sleep is affecting you into the day, and you dread the moment when you will lay your head down the next night, knowing your history with sleep has not been successful. This is an crucial moment to approach bedtime with a different attitude or continue to let your past dictate your future.

WHAT TO GET EXCITED ABOUT

- You get to strengthen your ability to be more enthusiastic than you feel.
- You have the opportunity to make a plan for the day that encourages sleep at night.
- This is a chance to find strength in God's grace and mercy.

STRENGTH THROUGH SCRIPTURE

- **Lamentations 3:23** "[His mercies] are new every morning."
- **Psalm 4:8** "I will both lie down in peace, and sleep; For You alone, O Lord, make me dwell in safety."
- **Proverbs 3:24** "When you lie down, you will not be afraid; Yes, you will lie down and your sleep will be sweet."

PRACTICAL WISDOM

1. *Avoid caffeine and other sleep inhibitors* – Sometimes a lack of sleep occurs as a result of simple behaviors. Pay attention to your caffeine habits. If you are drinking caffeine containing products after 5:00pm, it could be the culprit. Consuming sugar or starchy carbohydrates may play a part as well because they increase cortisol in your body. Avoid these sleep inhibitors and see if your rest improves.

2. *Find all-natural sleep solutions* – There are a number of nature-based sleep solutions available to people. There are sleep inducing teas containing lavender and chamomile, salt baths, natural sleep aids such as melatonin, and other natural remedies that aid is sleep. If you are not exercising, you may find that an hour of vigorous activity at some point in your day can help in the sleep process.

3. *See a doctor* – If you have tried everything you know to try and still have not found sleep, it may be a good idea to see a doctor. A doctor can access some of the possible causes of your sleeplessness and get you on track to a peaceful night's sleep. There are many specialized who are trained to identify and help solve sleep related problems.

DECLARATIONS

- God always shows up when I have trouble sleeping
- I am the best sleeper I know
- I go to sleep easily and wake up rested

CRUCIAL MOMENT

Simon and Hilda Groof are frustrated in their marriage. Simon complains there is not enough physical intimacy: "You are never in the mood. What is wrong with you?" Hilda longs for a deeper heart connection with Simon, but it hasn't been happening for years: "Simon, I don't feel close to you. I have heart needs that are going unmet. What is wrong with you?" If you have ever been at this fork in the road of marriage, then you know the decisions you make in this crucial moment are vital.

WHAT TO GET EXCITED ABOUT

- You get to understand in a deeper way how to say, "I love you" to your spouse in a way that he/she can "hear" it.

- You have the opportunity to understand the deep places in your spouse's heart like never before.

- This is a chance to see the supernatural released into your marriage to new levels.

STRENGTH THROUGH SCRIPTURE

- **Matthew 7:5** "First remove the plank from your own eye, and then you will see clearly to remove the speck from your brother's eye."

- **Ephesians 5:33** "Nevertheless let each one of you in particular so love his own wife as himself, and let the wife see that she respects her husband."

- **Matthew 6:33** "But seek first the kingdom of God and His righteousness, and all these things shall be added to you."

PRACTICAL WISDOM

1. *Actively pursue people and resources to improve what you bring to the marriage* – It is not a sign of weakness to realize how much you need help to be a good husband or wife. For instance, you don't need to be on the verge of divorce to get marriage counseling. Wisdom from others will help you navigate the unique aspects of your marriage. Also, we recommend you read, Danny Silk's book, *Keep Your Love On*. This will strengthen your connection, communication, and your boundaries in the relationship.

2. *Understand no person can meet our deepest needs* – If we expect a person to meet our deepest needs, then we will put unrealistic expectations on others that will further hinder our relationship. We will also live in frustration and disappointment which will block our ability to receive from the Lord, who is the one who can truly touch the deep heart needs of our lives. Try making a list of your deepest needs and delineate which ones were intended for God to meet. Give those areas of your life to Him.

3. *Realize the goal of marriage is not happiness* – Although happiness is a very real indicator of a healthy husband and wife relationship, marriage has a far more significant purpose than happiness. One of the by-products of marriage is for dysfunctions to rise to the surface of our lives so that we can experience God's healing and freedom.

DECLARATIONS

· God always shows up when my spouse is not meeting my needs.

· I have a satisfying and fulfilling marriage.

· I understand the legitimate needs of my spouse, and I am growing in meeting those needs.

CRUCIAL MOMENT

Obeying God looks different for each person. Many times, I feel God prompting me to step out in ways that challenge me and stretch me beyond my comfort zone. Whether it is speaking out a radical prophetic word, talking to a stranger in the grocery store line, or providing food for someone who is hungry, it always tests my ability to say, "Yes." I can sometimes allow the response of the person to determine whether I heard God correctly. When someone is not excited about my obedience, it is a crucial moment to see God show up.

WHAT TO GET EXCITED ABOUT

- It is impossible to obey God and for nothing to happen.
- Obedience is accredited to you as righteousness in God's sight.
- You get to increase in the raw faith it takes to say, "Yes," to God.

STRENGTH THROUGH SCRIPTURE

- **Isaiah 55:11** "So shall My word be that goes forth from My mouth; It shall not return to Me void, But it shall accomplish what I please, And it shall prosper in the thing for which I sent it."

- **Romans 4:20- 22** "He did not waver at the promise of God through unbelief, but was strengthened in faith, giving glory to God, and being fully convinced that what He had promised He was also able to perform. And therefore "it was accounted to him for righteousness."

- **2 Corinthians 5:7** "For we walk by faith, not by sight."

PRACTICAL WISDOM

1. *Focus on the positive* - Sometimes we are so focused on what didn't happen that we miss what did happen. God's idea of success is different from ours. When we give someone food who may have been asking for money, that person has a meal to eat. If we give a prophetic word that encourages someone, no matter how they receive it, encouragement goes a long way. Instead of paying attention to the negative, try focusing on the positives. The most significant victory is the act of obedience.

2. *Speak the truth* - It is hard to think a lie when speaking the truth. As we say things like, "God will honor my obedience," along with realizing that "If we don't live by the praises of man we won't die by their criticisms," fear of man breaks and boldness increases. Whenever you feel that your obedience might have been unfruitful, speak the truth over the situation and bless the person involved.

3. *Believe when you obey it commands a blessing* – The only person who knows whether or not you obeyed God is you. You are constantly faced with decisions and choices to say, "Yes," to God. God gives us promises in Scripture to encourage us. The promise connected to obedience is a blessing. No matter what happens outwardly, we know we serve a God who rewards obedience.

DECLARATIONS

- God always shows up when I obey Him and it looks unfruitful.
- My acts of obedience are storing up treasures in Heaven.
- I get excited when I have opportunities to obey God even if no person shows appreciation.

CRUCIAL MOMENT

You have family and friends who think you have joined a cult. They send you links to website articles on a daily basis which "expose" the false teachings and practices of your church to try to get you to see the error of your ways. Additionally, they send you videos of people associated with your ministry acting in bizarre ways to further prove their point. These family members and friends say you are being deceived. The initial reactions to this situation can be many and painful, but this crucial moment is an opportunity to grow in so many important parts of your life.

WHAT TO GET EXCITED ABOUT

- You get to nail down what you really believe Scripture says about key areas of doctrine that relate to other people's questions and concerns.
- You have the opportunity to decide your own path with God.
- This is a chance to grow in your love and wisdom toward those who are criticizing what you are doing.

STRENGTH THROUGH SCRIPTURE

- **Acts 17:11** "[The Bereans] received the word with all readiness, and searched the Scriptures daily to find out whether these things were so."
- **1 Corinthians 2:4-5** "And my speech and my preaching were not with persuasive words of human wisdom, but in demonstration of the Spirit and of power, that your faith should not be in the wisdom of men but in the power of God."
- **1 Thessalonians 5:19-22** " Do not quench the Spirit. Do not despise prophecies. Test all things; hold fast what is good. Abstain from every form of evil."

PRACTICAL WISDOM

1. *Believe and promote the basic doctrines of Scripture* – There are central beliefs in Christianity which cannot be compromised. These include: 1) The authority of the Scripture as the final word on all areas of life (2 Timothy 3:16-17). 2) The deity of Christ – Jesus is God (John 14:6), 3) The path of salvation and eternal life is through faith in Christ alone, not good works (Acts 4:12, Ephesians 2:8-9).

2. *Understand forerunner ministries and leaders are often criticized* – A study of church history reveals a pattern where times of spiritual revival were criticized and sometimes persecuted by those who were transformed by a previous revival. Almost every Christian denomination was thought to be heretical at first by those who did not embrace the new things being released. Most of these denominations now are considered orthodox in their beliefs and practices. Read articles or a book about church history in order to stir up faith in your current spiritual movement.

3. *Let your life be the best defense of the church or group you are a part of* – In 1 Peter 3:1, wives who have unbelieving husbands are told to live in such a way before that their husbands "may be won by the conduct of their wives." In other words, live in a way that wins the trust and respect of those you want to influence. As we interact with families and others who may have concerns about what we are a part of, realize the best answer to their questions is a transformed life of love, integrity, and purity. Avoid picking a fight or "proving" something. Your transformed life can often be the message that speaks loudest.

DECLARATIONS

- God always shows up when friends and family think my church is a cult.
- The Holy Spirit leads me in my interpretation of the Bible.
- I make powerful decisions regarding the ministries I connect with in my life.

46 YOU ARE IN RELATIONSHIP WITH A "ONE-UPPER" WHO HIJACKS YOUR STORIES

CRUCIAL MOMENT

You decide to tell a group of friends all about a life-changing experience you had while on vacation. The story is really good, and your friends are excited for the wonderful things in your life. As you are about to tell the best part of the whole experience, one of your good friends in the group interrupts you and says, "I remember when that happened to me. It was so cool." Your voice trails off into the background as she now has the attention of the entire group. Now, you start to feel like your story may not be that great after all. Feelings of resentment, frustration, and anger arise and you realize that this person does this to you and others often. We all know people like this. Whether they are trying to outdo your story or genuinely just want to share about themselves, they negatively affect you with each hijacked story. It is in this moment that you have a decision to make.

WHAT TO GET EXCITED ABOUT

- You get to self-evaluate and understand your needs to a higher level.
- You have the opportunity to evaluate how to handle difficult relationships in your life with love.
- This is a chance to communicate how someone else is affecting you in important situations.

STRENGTH THROUGH SCRIPTURE

- **Matthew 7:5** "First remove the plank from your own eye, and then you will see clearly to remove the speck from your brother's eye."
- **Galatians 5:23** "The fruits of the Spirit are .... gentleness, self-control. Against such there is no law."
- **Matthew 18:15** "Moreover if your brother sins against you, go and tell him his fault between you and him alone. If he hears you, you have gained your brother."

PRACTICAL WISDOM

1. *Assess your emotions* – Not feeling heard can be a problem in a relationship. You may think that stuffing it or pretending that you are unaffected by the actions of another is dealing with it, but it will only work for so long. When you realize that you are negatively affected by the "one-upper," take a moment and assess your emotions. It might seem small or unimportant, but your relationship is important. If you are being negatively affected by them and cannot find a solution in your heart, it could be time for a conversation.

2. *Believe the best* – There are many reasons why people do this. Some do it intentionally, but for the most part, many are unaware they are causing a problem. In any relational situation, it is important to believe the best about the person and their intentions. When someone hurts you or causes you discomfort in any way, take a moment and say this to yourself, "I know they would never want to hurt me. I feel hurt, but that was not their intention." Once you find a place of peace, make a plan for talking to them about it if you still feel it is necessary.

3. *Consider communicating in private* – Personalities and depth of relationship are important to consider when addressing the situation. For some people, you can address it immediately by saying, "Hey, can I finish my story and then you can share?" But, this won't work for everyone. If you are in a group of people, it is probably not the best time to talk to the "one-upper" about the issue. They may be insecure, trying to fit in, or just unaware of what is going on. If you call someone out in a group setting, it can cause more harm than good and embarrass both of you. Instead, find a time where you can talk to them privately about how their actions are affecting you. Remember to use "I feel" statements. These go like this: I feel _____ when you _____. I know you would never want to hurt me, but I feel _____. Can you help me understand?

DECLARATIONS

- God always shows up when I am in relationship with a one-upper.
- I am self-controlled and in charge of my responses to the actions of others.
- I am honoring, and I love to cover those who I am in relationship with.

47 YOUR EXPENSES ARE GREATER THAN YOUR INCOME

CRUCIAL MOMENT

Your finances are fully occupying your thoughts. You simply don't have enough money to pay your bills, keep food on the table, or gas in the car. This is a pivotal moment where God has not only shown up for countless people before you, but also promises to do so for you!

WHAT TO GET EXCITED ABOUT

- You get to trust God, going deeper into a relationship with Him and His miraculous tendencies as He loves on you through divine provision.
- You have the opportunity to grow your testimony, telling of how God spoke to you in your time of need.
- This is a chance to find peace as you realize that you have been given a new and divine solution to your financial problems.

STRENGTH THROUGH SCRIPTURE

- **Matthew 6:25** "Therefore I say to you, do not worry about your life, what you will eat or what you will drink; nor about your body, what you will put on. Is not life more than food and the body more than clothing?"
- **Philippians 4:6** "Be anxious for nothing, but in everything by prayer and supplication, with thanksgiving, let your requests be made known to God."
- **1 Peter 5:7** "casting all your care upon Him, for He cares for you."

PRACTICAL WISDOM

1. *Remove fear and feelings of abandonment* – Indeed, we are sons and daughters of the King. When we desire for the Holy Spirit to move in supernatural solutions or provision, we make our minds a welcoming place for Him, which is a place swept clean of fear and doubt. Tell those close to you that they have permission to boldy let you know when your words and perspectives feel driven by fear, irrational concern, and worry. Soon, you'll be able to catch your thoughts at the root and become a place the Holy Spirit can reside throughout the day!

2. *Give* – Find someone who is in even more need than you, and give to them. Give generously. Not only is this a prophetic act of your faith in God, but also you are making God an offer that He promises not to ignore! It's a spiritual law. Check out Luke 6:38. "Give, and it will be given to you..."

3. *Take on the mindset of a solution-finder* – Though you're in need of financial provision, you have other spiritual assets that others need. God is a good God and lets us be part of each other's solutions. He will often have us meet someone who needs a solution... a solution that God, through us, will provide to them. Sometimes, this person may be part of your solution for finances. God loves to bring his kids not only provision, but upgrades at the same time.

DECLARATIONS

- God always shows up when I don't have enough money to pay my bills.
- My life is dripping with abundance.
- I am trustworthy with money. God trusts me with His resources.

A PERSON IN YOUR LIFE HAS A HABIT OF SAYING NEGATIVE THINGS ABOUT OTHERS

CRUCIAL MOMENT

Elsie is a friend of yours. She is fun and outgoing and is a lively conversationalist. You like her, but she has a habit of slipping in negative comments about others when she is trying to be funny or when she is verbally processing through what is happening in her life. She does not blatantly gossip or slander, but it becomes clear when she does not hold someone in the highest regard. You want to keep your friendship, but you realize that if she is saying these things to you about others, she is probably saying similar things to others about you. You are not sure what to do.

WHAT TO GET EXCITED ABOUT

- You get to learn how to keep your beliefs strong regarding people about whom you hear negative things.

- You have the opportunity to reassess whether or not you are a person who attracts gossip and negative comments about others.

- This is a chance to strengthen your brave communication skills.

STRENGTH THROUGH SCRIPTURE

- **Colossians 3:12-13** "Therefore, as the elect of God, holy and beloved, put on tender mercies, kindness, humility, meekness, longsuffering; bearing with one another, and forgiving one another."

- **Proverbs 26:22** "The words of a talebearer are like tasty trifles, and they go down into the inmost body."

- **1 Timothy 5:19** "Do not receive an accusation against an elder except from two or three witnesses."

PRACTICAL WISDOM

1. ***Be very careful what you say about others*** – It is the wise person who errs on the side of caution when talking about others in group settings or in one-on-one conversations. This is especially true if we are talking about someone who has hurt us or disappointed us. If we become known as a person who does not criticize others in conversation, then it is less likely others will come to us with negativity about someone else. Give people in your life permission to let you know when you are talking negatively about others.

2. ***Realize people lose trust in someone who talks negatively about others*** – When we hear someone not being careful in speech about others, we will conclude (consciously or unconsciously) they will not be careful in what they say about us to others. This realization should create a healthy caution in our relationships with those who do not protect the reputations of others in what they say. Make declarations over yourself about being a trustworthy person who speaks in an honoring way about others.

3. ***Learn how to not receive negative hearsay information about others*** – 1 Timothy 5:19 says to not "receive" an unsubstantiated negative word about a leader. We can reject receiving hearsay information about leaders or anyone else by: 1) Not allowing it to influence our opinion of the one spoken about. 2) Saying something positive about the person to the negative speaker. 3) Sharing with the careless talker that you feel uncomfortable hearing things like that about others.

DECLARATIONS

- God always shows up when someone around me talks negatively about others.

- I build up the people in my life with my words.

- I am a person who has powerful beliefs about others.

CRUCIAL MOMENT

You and a fellow leader in your church cannot agree on how to handle a tense and troublesome situation. You believe strongly that you know what to do, but he thinks that it is the wrong approach to take. You've butted heads in team meetings, and when you have met in private, you still seem miles apart on coming into agreement. You are frustrated that he is not seeing the big picture, and you are concerned a bad decision is going to cause some real problems. You value the relationship, so you know it is important how you navigate the situation from here.

WHAT TO GET EXCITED ABOUT

* You get to learn how to walk in love and joy when there are unresolved situations in relationships.
* You have the opportunity to exhibit honor in a challenging relationship.
* This is a chance to hear God's wisdom about what you should do.

STRENGTH THROUGH SCRIPTURE

* **Romans 12:18** "If it is possible, as much as depends on you, live peaceably with all men."
* **Acts 15:39-40** "Then the contention became so sharp that they parted from one another. And so Barnabas took Mark and sailed to Cyprus, but Paul chose Silas and departed, being commended by the brethren to the grace of God."
* **1 Corinthians 13:4-7** "Love suffers long and is kind; love does not envy; love does not parade itself, is not puffed up; does not behave rudely, does not seek its own, is not provoked, thinks no evil; does not rejoice in iniquity, but rejoices in the truth; bears all things, believes all things, hopes all things, endures all things."

PRACTICAL WISDOM

1. *Realize the relationship is almost always more important than the disagreement* – 1 Corinthians 13 affirms the priority of loving attitudes and actions in our lives. It points us toward a lifestyle of prioritizing relational love above spiritual gifts, mountain-moving faith, giving to the poor, and even above martyrdom (see I Corinthians 13:1-3). We are to do all we can do to "live peaceably with all men." If we are a person committed to love and to understanding those with whom we are in disagreement, then when we need to leave or set a boundary in a relationship, we will have a much greater likelihood of being correct in the direction we take.

2. *Implement these steps to increase the likelihood of resolving the disagreement* – 1) Pray- "You do not have, because you do not ask" (James 4:2). 2) Humble yourself - seek forgiveness of any wrongs you have done. 3) Avoid talking negatively about this person to others. Many have compounded disagreements by sharing too much information with people who have no business knowing about your difference of opinion. 4) Meet with an impartial person who is full of the Holy Spirit and wisdom, trusting God to work through this process.

3. *Learn how to disagree agreeably* – We have to choose our battles carefully, and we do not always have to be right. We also don't have to label people who disagree with us as our enemy. Powerful people still honor when there is a dispute. They avoid reactive language like "You always," "You never," or "You are stupid." We know we are growing up when we still seek to keep heart connections with people when we don't see eye to eye with them (even if we have to eventually go our separate ways).

DECLARATIONS

- God always shows up when a significant person in my life disagrees with me about something important.

- I don't need to have agreement with everyone to thrive in life.

- I have a unique ability to resolve disagreements in my relationships.

50 A FAMILY MEMBER IS AN ATHEIST AND PROUD OF IT

CRUCIAL MOMENT

Every time you are at a family function, one family member decides to relentlessly promote his beliefs that God is not real. Not only that, he makes personal attacks on your decision to follow Christ with your life and career. This has been happening for years, and practicing the method of "turning the other cheek" doesn't seem to be working anymore. You have ignored him, laughed at his jokes, and even had a discussion about how his behavior is affecting you, but he does not seem to care. It is during this crucial moment that you get to decide how you are going to continue in relationship to this person.

WHAT TO GET EXCITED ABOUT

- Self-control is a fruit of the Spirit and this is a good opportunity to practice it.
- You get to learn how to set boundaries and not be emotionally manipulated by people.
- This is an opportunity to give grace.

STRENGTH THROUGH SCRIPTURE

- **2 Corinthians 13:11** "Finally, brethren, farewell. Become complete. Be of good comfort, be of one mind, live in peace; and the God of love and peace will be with you."
- **Proverbs 22:11** "He who loves purity of heart and has grace on his lips, the King will be his friend."
- **Proverbs 25:21-22** "If your enemy is hungry, give him bread to eat; and if he is thirsty, give him water to drink; for so you will heap coals of fire on his head, and the Lord will reward you.

PRACTICAL WISDOM

1. *Kindness is good medicine* – No matter how many times you turn the other cheek, kindness is still good medicine. When it comes to ideological and philosophical beliefs, each person must come to a decision themselves. You cannot force someone to believe like you, but you can be an example and display the kindness and love of God no matter what they do. This may not be easy, but it will be a testimony of your commitment to the message of love over and over again.

2. *Bravely Communicate the need for resolution* – If your family member takes the pestering too far, it might be a good time to practice communicating your goal in resolving the conflict. You can choose to understand one another without having to agree on the same thing or needing to convince the other person that you are right and they are wrong. If your goal is understanding, then you will be able to communicate what you need from the conversation.

3. *Sow seeds for supernatural encounter* – Prayer changes things. It is impossible to pray and nothing happen. When you pray, you are given an opportunity to sow seeds of faith into the atmosphere. No person is too far away that they cannot be saved, and God has a heart that all people would come to salvation. Imagine what it would be like for your family member to be transformed by the love of God. See them through the eyes of Christ and know that nothing is impossible with Him.

DECLARATIONS

- God always shows up when a family member declares he is an atheist.
- My prayers for my family members are powerful and effective.
- I release grace and peace over the people in my life.

51 YOU ARE STRUGGLING WITH AN ADDICTIVE BEHAVIOR

CRUCIAL MOMENT

You find yourself doing what you don't want to do, and not doing what you desire to do, just like the description the Apostle Paul makes in Romans 7. You have tried to overcome a certain habit, but it seems to be a losing battle. With each seeming failure in your fight against addiction, you feel like you are taking another lap around a desert filled with hopelessness and shame. This habit is hurting your relationships with others, and nothing you have done has seemed to work for more than a few days. Moments like this provide a chance to get addicted to the God who sets you free.

WHAT TO GET EXCITED ABOUT

- You get to learn how to receive God's unconditional love even when you are struggling.

- You have the opportunity to realize again that your hopelessness about a problem is a bigger problem than the problem, and you are given the opportunity to intentionally change the way you think.

- This is a chance to be positioned to bring incredible freedom to others who struggle in the same area as you.

STRENGTH THROUGH SCRIPTURE

- **1 Corinthians 10:13** "No temptation has overtaken you except such as is common to man; but God is faithful, who will not allow you to be tempted beyond what you are able, but with the temptation will also make the way of escape, that you may be able to bear it."

- **Romans 6:11** "Likewise you also, reckon yourselves to be dead indeed to sin, but alive to God in Christ Jesus our Lord."

- **2 Corinthians 12:9-10** "'My grace is sufficient for you, for My strength is made perfect in weakness.' Therefore most gladly I will rather boast in my infirmities (weaknesses), that the power of Christ may rest upon me. Therefore I take pleasure in infirmities, in reproaches, in needs, in persecutions, in distresses, for Christ's sake. For when I am weak, then I am strong.'"

PRACTICAL WISDOM

1. *Know you cannot consistently do what you don't believe you are* – The life of faith believes we are something before we ever experience it. We are to believe and then see, not see then believe. If we try to act in a manner which is inconsistent with our core beliefs about ourselves, then our beliefs will become the biggest problem in changing what we do. As we renew our minds with truth about our identity in Christ, our behavior will be transformed (Romans 12:2).

2. *Pursue empowering relationships* – Those who realize they need others will be more victorious in life. All of us seem to have at least one area in life where we need the involvement of friends or skilled people. This is crucial to our well-being. This need for other peoples' support helps us live a life of humility and to prioritize relationships. When we ask God to help us, He usually sends anointed and gifted people into our lives. Truly, we need each other.

3. *Realize your battle is not just about you, but about everyone you will influence in the future* – Our life passions and ministry emphasis often come from the areas in which we have overcome. My emphasis of hope and joy results from great victories over discouragement and "joy-impairedness." When I was battling for breakthrough in my life, I did not realize my battle was more about others than it was about me. It is the same for you now. You are called to increasing influence. Your freedom will bring freedom to many others. It is indeed part of your life purpose.

DECLARATIONS

- God always shows up when I am battling an addictive behavior.

- I have quality relationships with strong, addiction-free people.

- My breakthrough will influence many others to find freedom in this area of life.

52 SOMEONE PRAISES YOU FOR YOUR ACCOMPLISHMENTS

CRUCIAL MOMENT

You've heard the tragic story of a star athlete, musician, or favorite minister who had so much talent and charisma, capturing the attention of many, yet somehow ended up becoming a "one hit wonder." Though everyone loved and worshipped them for a season, their life seemed to fall by the wayside. What happened? Somewhere along the line it seems like all the attention started adversely affecting their perception of themselves. How do you respond when people praise you for your accomplishments? Do you become impressed with yourself? Do you deflect praise, minimizing your efforts? Or, do you get excited, knowing that God always shows up when people praise you?

WHAT TO GET EXCITED ABOUT

- You get a "bigger crown" to throw at Jesus' feet (Revelation 4:10).

- You have the opportunity to face a test which will lead to discovering more of what is in your heart.

- This is a chance to learn how to receive a compliment while not letting it define who you are.

STRENGTH THROUGH SCRIPTURE

- **Proverbs 27:21** "The crucible for silver and the furnace for gold, but people are tested by their praise." (NIV)

- **1 Peter 5:6** "Therefore humble yourselves under the mighty hand of God, that He may exalt you in due time."

- **1 Corinthians 4:7** "For who makes you differ from another? And what do you have that you did not receive? Now if you did indeed receive it, why do you boast as if you had not received it?"

PRACTICAL WISDOM

1. *Remind yourself that God is the one who gives you all your abilitiesc* - No matter what you do, or what your capabilities are, choose to believe that without Him you can do nothing. Everything good in your life comes from God. Keeping this realization at the forefront of your mind will help you in responding graciously to the praises of men.

2. *Refuse to find your identity in what people say about you* - Recognition is something that every person desires. However, if our lives are fueled by the praises of men, we will find it difficult to move forward when public recognition is scarce, and we will likely experience a meltdown when spoken of negatively. Find your identity in what God says about you, not what people say about you.

3. *Resolve to live a lifestyle of worship, thankfulness, and intimacy with God*- God is looking for a generation that He can entrust the entire world to. However, as much as He desires to lavishly bless and promote you, He loves you and your long-term well-being more. His blessings to you will often increase to the degree you can steward them. For example, He doesn't give 10 cities to someone who has been unfaithful with one mina (read Luke 19:11-27). This would be cruel as it would be setting them up to fail. A generation is arising that is so fascinated with Him that the things of this world (notoriety, wealth, etc.) mean nothing in comparison.

DECLARATIONS

- God always shows up when others praise me for my accomplishments.

- I receive compliments easily and can smile knowing that my Father is the One who made it possible for me to do all things.

- I am not defined by what I do, but by who God says I am.

ADDITIONAL RESOURCES

Victorious Mindsets

What we believe is ultimately more important than what we do. The course of our lives is set by our deepest core beliefs. Our mindsets are either a stronghold for God's purposes or a playhouse for the enemy. In this book, fifty biblical attitudes are revealed that are foundational for those who desire to walk in freedom and power.

Cracks in the Foundation

Going to a higher level in establishing key beliefs will affect ones intimacy with God and fruitfulness for the days ahead. This book challenges many basic assumptions of familiar Bible verses and common Christian phrases that block numerous benefits of our salvation. The truths shared in this book will help fill and repair "cracks" in our thinking which rob us of our God-given potential.

You're Crazy If You Don't Talk to Yourself

Jesus did not just think His way out of the wilderness and neither can we. He spoke truth to invisible beings and mindsets that sought to restrict and defeat Him. This book reveals that life and death are truly in the power of the tongue, and emphasize the necessity of speaking truth to our souls. Our words really do set the course of our lives and the lives of others. (Proverbs 18:21; James 3:2-5)

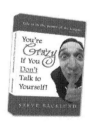

Let's Just Laugh at That

Our hope level is an indicator of whether we are believing truth or lies. Truth creates hope and freedom, but believing lies brings hopelessness and restriction. We can have great theology but still be powerless because of deception about the key issues of life. Many of these self-defeating mindsets exist in our subconscious and have never been identified. This

book exposes numerous falsehoods and reveals truth that makes us free. Get ready for a joy-infused adventure into hope-filled living.

Divine Strategies for Increase

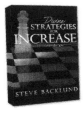

The laws of the spirit are more real than the natural laws. God's laws are primarily principles to release blessing, not rules to be obeyed to gain right standing with God. The Psalmist talks of one whose greatest delight is in the law of the Lord. This delight allows one to discover new aspects of the nature of God (hidden in each law) to behold and worship. The end result of this delighting is a transformed life that prospers in every endeavor. His experience can be our experience, and this book unlocks the blessings hidden in the spiritual realm.

Possessing Joy

In His presence is fullness of joy (Psalm 16:11). Joy is to increase as we go deeper in our relationship with God. Religious tradition has devalued the role that gladness and laughter have for personal victory and Kingdom advancement. His presence may not always produce joy; but if we never or rarely have fullness of joy, we must reevaluate our concept of God. This book takes one on a journey toward the headwaters of the full joy that Jesus often spoke of. Get ready for joy to increase and strength and longevity to ignite.

Igniting Faith in 40 Days

There must be special seasons in our lives when we break out of routine and do something that will ignite our faith about God and our identity in Christ. This book will lead you through the life-changing experience of a 40-day negativity fast. This fast teaches the power of declaring truth and other transforming daily customs that will strengthen your foundation of faith and radically increase your personal hope.

Living From The Unseen

This book will help you identify beliefs that block the reception of God's blessings and hinder our ability to live out our destiny. This book reveals that 1) Believing differently, not trying harder, is the key to change; 2) You cannot do what you don't believe you are; 3) You can only receive what you think you are worth; 4) Rather than learning how to die — it is time to learn how to live.

Declarations

"Nothing happens in the Kingdom unless a declaration is made." Believers everywhere are realizing the power of declarations to empower their lives. You may be wondering, "What are declarations and why are people making them?" or maybe, "Aren't declarations simply a repackaged 'name it and claim' heresy?" Declarations answers these questions by sharing 30 biblical reasons for declaring truth over every area of life. Steve Backlund and his team also answer common objections and concerns to the teaching about declarations. The revelation this book carries will help you to set the direction your life will go. Get ready for 30 days of powerful devotions and declarations that will convince you that life is truly in the power of the tongue.

Audio message series are available through the Igniting Hope store at: *www.IgnitingHope.com*

ADDITIONAL RESOURCES FROM STEVE AND WENDY BACKLUND

53885083R00068

Made in the USA
Charleston, SC
18 March 2016